Down Memory Lane

Topics and Ideas for Reminiscence Groups

by

Beckie Karras
Registered Music Therapist-Board Certified
Activities Consultant Certified

Illustrations by Nancy Abood Briefs

© 1985 Rebecca Poling Karras

All rights reserved. No part of this book may be reproduced without permission of the author, except where specifically need for clinical use.

First printing 1985 • Second printing, 1986
Third printing 1986 • Fourth printing, 1988
Fifth printing 1989 • Sixth printing 1991
Seventh printing 1992 • Eighth printing 1993
Ninth printing 1994

For additional copies or a free catalog of other products, write to the publisher:

P.O. Box 74
Mt. Airy, Maryland 21771

Printed in the U.S.A. by G & H Printing, Mt. Airy, Maryland

ISBN 1-879633-00-0

DEDICATION

This book is lovingly dedicated to the memory of my grandmother, Mary Wine Smith, who inspired me to love, and to want to spend my life with, older people.

ACKNOWLEDGEMENTS

I want to express my deep appreciation...

...to my dear husband Phil, for his ideas, technical expertise, and unwavering belief in this project;

...to my parents, Newton and Virginia Poling, for the historical and editorial knowledge they shared and the excitement they showed for the work;

...and to the residents of Bethesda Retirement and Nursing Center, who tested the programs and shared so many memories.

Contents

Introduction 1

Advertisements 4
Advice 7
American Popular Song 10
Big Bands 16
Broadway Musicals 20
Childhood 24
Comedians 28
Dancing 32
Fashions 36
The Funnies 39
The Golden Age of Television 43
Home Sweet Home 47
Ice Cream Parlor 51
The Movies 55
Moving Along 59
My Home Town 63
Needlework 66
The News 69
Old-time Radio 73
Opera 77
Operetta 81
Pets 84
Photographs 87
The Roaring Twenties 89
Roosevelt and the Thirties 93
School Days 98
Shopping 103

Sports 106
Superstitions 110
Vacations 113
Vaudeville 117
Voices from the Past 121
Weddings 125
Working 128

APPENDIX A - ANNOTATED RESOURCE LIST 131
APPENDIX B - INDEX TO POPULAR SONGS 134
APPENDIX C - QUIZ AND GAME INDEX 138

INTRODUCTION

This book is based on a series of sessions called "Down Memory Lane" that I originated in the nursing home where I have worked since 1978. When I held the first one, I told the residents that it would be "the first in an irregular series of lighthearted sessions for remembering the good old days." I expected the groups to have about 15-20 people in them each time. However, they quickly became so popular that we soon had almost twice that number attending, with rave reviews after each session. (In spite of this success, I believe that smaller groups are preferable. I was fortunate to have the help of a staff member and a good sound system, so that a large group was manageable.) After doing sessions for a year, the one on radio was so well received that I decided to share my ideas with other activity people, hence this book.

Although prepared for use in nursing or retirement homes, these programs could be easily adapted for use with older adults wherever they meet—in community senior citizen organizations, adult daycare centers, senior church groups, residential care facilities, etc.

Each chapter has been written so that there are enough ideas to have a successful session, even with very limited resources. The sessions can be as simple or as complex as you want, depending on how much you try to do in a single session. I always prepared for more than enough to fill a 45-minute session because it was difficult to predict in advance what would most spark the participants' reminiscing. Most of the chapters have enough ideas for more than one session if you want to do a short series.

Each chapter has also been written so that it is possible to do sessions without a great deal of preparation and research on the topic. However, the more you know ahead of time and the more audio-visual aids you use, the more stimulating the sessions will be.

There are three sections that make up each chapter:

1. **IN THE MOOD**. These are suggestions for relevant music and visual aids that will set the mood and enhance the theme, that will give people something to talk about as they enter, and that will stimulate discussion within the session.

2. **ACTIVITIES**. These vary greatly with each theme but can be a quiz game; viewing and discussing relevant pictures or objects; seeing a film; a demonstration of how to do something; having guest speakers; listening to recorded excerpts of music or speeches; singing; or having the participants take part in doing something. There is usually a suggestion on how to link the topic to today's world. (I have found that the participants are usually interested in these because they are eager to learn about new things.) There are many suggestions for appropriate ways to begin and/or end a session. And there are suggestions for other activities that relate to the theme but that are not strictly reminiscence or that are major activities in themselves. (Listed as "Related Activities.")

3. **DISCUSSION**. These are broader questions that will stimulate further discussion and encourage the residents to share more memories. These questions can be used to begin the session, throughout the session, or all at the end, whichever you prefer.

These three sections can be combined or intertwined, depending on the subject and on your own personal style. It is hoped that there are enough ideas and suggestions in each chapter to stimulate your own creative abilities in designing programs that will suit your group and the materials you have available.

These programs can be adapted for use with different sizes of groups. A small group (10-12, or less) can focus on a more specific topic and more participants will probably be willing to join in the discussion, to tell longer stories, and to take part in the activities. A large group (25-30) can be successful by asking many questions with short answers and then asking individual participants to elaborate on broader questions. Some of the reminiscing in a large group will take place among two to three participants sitting together and in the conversations the participants have as they leave the activity area.

Suggestions on the use of music and visual aids:

1. When playing music as the participants enter, be aware of the volume. If too soft, no one will be able to hear it. If too loud, the participants will be unable to socialize.

2. If you don't have enough music to play for the 15-30 minutes as the participants enter, try to find at least one piece of music to play or to sing that will set the mood at the beginning of the session and will introduce the topic.

3. If using recorded music, tapes or compact discs are usually the easiest to use, but the inconvenience of a record player is preferable to using a small tape recorder that can't be heard or understood or that has poor sound quality. Consider the size of your room and the quality of your equipment when deciding which to use.

4. A good way to start each session is to talk briefly about what visual aids or music you've found or to ask a leading question from the Discussion section.

5. To keep the flow of the program going, especially in a larger group, it will be helpful if you can have a volunteer, another staff member, or a participant who will help pass around any objects or pictures you have to show.

6. A microphone is very helpful in a large group, not only so that the residents can hear you but so that the residents can hear each other. If you have no microphone, repeat what residents have shared so all can hear.

There is an Annotated Resource List (Appendix A) in the back of the book for suggestions on where to find appropriate objects, pictures, and music. Appendix B is an index of popular songs and the years they were written or popularized, from 1892 to 1949. Appendix C is a quick reference index to the many quizzes and games found in the book.

In doing publicity for the session, you could tell the participants the topic and ask them to share an object or a memory when they come, or you could give the participants a question to think about before coming. By letting the participants know the topic in advance, they may already have some memories in mind to share. On the other hand, if you have some excellent audio-visual aids available for a session, you could challenge the participants to guess what the topic is for that day.

I found that the best endings for my sessions used some humor: a joke, a cartoon or comic strip, an outlandish invention, something futuristic, or a human interest story that is relevant to your topic. These could be from you or from the participants. I have sometimes asked the participants early in a session to think of a good story that could be told at the end. And of course, serving refreshments or singing a well-known song is a great way to end, too.

The older people with whom we work have a wealth of memories to share and it is exciting to create an atmosphere where the past can live again for them.

Beckie Karras
August 1985

ADVERTISEMENTS

IN THE MOOD

Music Possibilities

1. Famous jingles: "I'd Like to Teach the World to Sing" (Coca-Cola); Chiquita Banana song; Java Coffee song. Also, Barry Manilow has put together a medley of his best-known jingles.

2. Recordings of advertisements: If you have recordings of any old radio shows, there will usually be an ad during the show, often incorporated into the story line. You could play one of these radio shows as people come in, or you could tape excerpts from several shows. Presta Sounds has a 60-minute tape of advertisements, "Reminiscing through Commercials." (See Appendix A.) If you have none of these recordings, you can play big band music to remind participants of the decades to which you will be referring.

Visual Possibilities

1. Cut ads from magazines (preferably in color), mount on construction paper, and display in the activity room. You may also give an ad to each participant who attends. Try to find ads for products that were first sold between 1920 and 1940, e.g., Morton's Salt, Maxwell House Coffee, Sherwin-Williams Paint, Coca-Cola, Ivory Soap. (See also the lists of products in Activities #3, 4, and 7.) If you have access to some very old magazines, you can display original ads. You can find ads in *Good Old Days* magazine and your library should have books about advertising. (See also Dover Publications' *American Trademark Designs*.)

2. If you have a nearby antique dealer, the owner may let you borrow some old advertising objects, such as for Coca-Cola.

3. Write some of the slogans from Activity #3 on banners and display in the activity room. You might want to make a Burma Shave ad in the hallway leading to the activity room. (Burma Shave had a series of signs, on the highways, with a line of a funny poem on each sign and Burma Shave on the final sign.) Examples:

"Every shaver/now can snore/six more minutes/than before/ by using/Burma Shave"
"Does your husband/misbehave/grunt and grumble/rant and rave?/Shoot the brute some/Burma Shave"
"The 50-cent jar/so large/by heck/even the Scotch/now shave the neck/Burma Shave"

ACTIVITIES

1. **Magazine Ads.** Read the slogans you cut from the magazines and see if the participants remember what other slogans were used by these companies, or how else they might have advertised their product. (Participants may read the ads aloud, if able.) Ask the participants what they thought of each product—was it good or not worth buying?

2. **Commercials.** If you have recordings of several old commercials, play them for the participants. Ask them what the product was and if any of them ever used it.

3. **Sponsors.** Some of the participants may remember what radio show was sponsored by which company:

      Jack Benny - **Jello or Lucky Strike**
      Edgar Bergen and Charlie McCarthy - **Chase & Sanborn Coffee**
      Burns and Allen - **Maxwell House Coffee**
      Jimmy Durante - **Rexall Drug Stores**
      Little Orphan Annie - **Ovaltine**
      Fibber McGee and Molly - **Johnson's Wax**
      Your Hit Parade - **Lucky Strike Cigarettes**

4. **Slogans.** Name the slogan and have the participants name the product:

Ask the man who owns one. **Packard**
Babies cry for it. **Castoria**
They satisfy. **Chesterfield**
Covers the earth. **Sherwin-Williams Paint**
His master's voice. **Victrola**
The pause that refreshes. **Coca-Cola**
The breakfast of champions. **Wheaties**
57 varieties. **Heinz**
The skin you love to touch. **Woodbury**
Hasn't scratched yet. **Bon Ami**

99 44/100 percent pure. **Ivory Soap**
Time to re-tire. **Fisk Tires**
From contented cows. **Carnation Milk**
Chases dirt. **Old Dutch Cleanser**
Keep that schoolgirl complexion. **Palmolive**
When it rains it pours. **Morton's Salt**
Good to the last drop. **Maxwell House Coffee**
You can be sure if it's. . .**Westinghouse**
Makes clothes sparkle. **Oxydol**
Candy mint with the hole. **Life Savers**

5. Offer each participant a small glass of Coca-Cola, served in a Coke cup if you can find them.

Down Memory Lane

6. **Promotional Products.** Look around your home. You may find an object that is clearly an advertisement or promotion for something. Share it with the participants and tell how you obtained it. Examples: Star Wars glasses, slogan tee shirts, Mickey Mouse watch. Ask the participants if they ever owned anything similar that promoted a product. (Many radio shows gave away promotional products.) Ask them if they remember all the different places that Coca-Cola advertising could be found (soda fountains, billboards, storefront windows, Coke glasses, Coke trays.)

7. **Trademarks.** Name the following trademarks and ask the participants to name the product:

> An aristocratic tomato man. **Heinz**
> A Dutch girl holding up a washing stick. **Old Dutch Cleanser**
> A boy in a yellow raincoat and hat. **Uneeda Biscuit**
> A girl in a raincoat standing under an umbrella. **Morton Salt**
> A smoking penguin. **Kool Cigarettes**
> Elsie the Cow. **Borden's Milk**
> A metal tin in the shape of a log cabin. **Log Cabin Syrup**
> An Indian maiden. **Land O' Lakes Butter**
> A bellboy, calling out. **Philip Morris Cigarettes**
> A dog by a phonograph. **Victrola**
> A newly hatched yellow chick. **Bon Ami Scouring Powder**

8. **Creating a Slogan.** If your group likes a challenge, ask them to imagine that they are responsible for promoting a product or a company and need to make up a slogan and/or a trademark for it. Pick a product or company with which they are familiar but that doesn't already have a well-known slogan. It could be something local or even a promotion for your town or your facility. Have the participants make a list of all its positive attributes, using as many adjectives as possible. (Write these so that all can see.) Then pick one or two of these attributes to highlight for your slogan.

DISCUSSION

1. How did you decide what products to buy for your home? Did you ever buy something just because: Your mother or mother-in-law used it? You heard it advertised? You experimented with products and picked the best ones? You bought the most or the least expensive? Your spouse or children wanted the product? There was a free gift offer that came with it?

2. Does advertising bother any of you, do you ignore it, or do you think it serves a useful purpose?

3. Do any of you remember how "soap operas" got that name? (Sponsored by soap companies.)

4. Did any of you do all the buying for your family?

5. Did any of you ever own or work in a business that involved selling? Do you remember what the wholesalers did to encourage you to sell their products? Did you ever advertise?

6. Did any of you ever work as a sales representative? What did you sell? Did you do anything special to get people to buy your product?

IN THE MOOD

Music Possibilities - Songs giving advice. Examples:

"Pack up your Troubles in Your Old Kit Bag"
"Don't Sit Under the Apple Tree"
"Young at Heart"
"Button Up Your Overcoat"
"Smile"
"People will Say We're in Love"
"Swinging on a Star"
"Let a Smile be your Umbrella"
"You'll Never Walk Alone"
"Keep Your Sunny Side Up"
"Oh Lady Be Good"
"Look for the Silver Lining"

"Count Your Blessings"
"Whistle a Happy Tune"
"Pennies from Heaven"
"On the Sunny Side of the Street"
"16 Going on 17"
"Try a Little Tenderness"
"Get Happy"
"Wait till the Sun Shines, Nellie"
"High Hopes"
"Ac-cent-tchu-ate the Positive"
"Climb Every Mountain"

Visual Possibilities - Write some short sayings on posters with bold, black markers and place around the room. (See Activity #2.) If you have time, put appropriate pictures on the posters, e.g., a picture of chickens with "Don't count your chickens before they hatch."

ACTIVITIES

1. **Advice Songs**. Ask the participants if they can think of the names of some songs giving advice. Then sing some advice songs.

2. **Common Sayings**. Ask the participants to name any advice or common sayings that they remember. Have the participants then complete the following common sayings:

> Absence makes the heart. . .**grow fonder**.
> Out of sight. . .**out of mind**.
> Birds of a feather. . .**flock together**.
> Beauty is. . .**skin deep**.
> The early bird. . .**gets the worm**.
> A new broom. . .**sweeps clean**.
> A penny saved is. . .**a penny earned**.
> Haste makes. . .**waste**.
> It's better to be safe. . .**than sorry**.
> Children should be seen. . .**and not heard**.
> Spare the rod and. . .**spoil the child**.
> Too many cooks. . .**spoil the broth**.
> Make hay while. . .**the sun shines**.
> You can't teach an old dog. . .**new tricks**.
> Familiarity breeds. . .**contempt**.
> There's no fool. . .**like an old fool**.
> Marry in haste and. . .**repent at leisure**.
> Two heads are. . .**better than one**.
> A bird in the hand is worth. . .**two in the bush**.
> Rolling stones . . .**gather no moss**.

You could also write uncompleted sayings in largeprint on slips of paper and give one to each participant. Have each participant read his or her saying for other participants to complete. For a longer list of sayings, use *Memories, Dreams and Thoughts* or *The Fun Encyclopedia*. (See Appendix A.)

3. **Confused Sayings**. Divide several sayings in two parts. Write the first part on one slip of paper and the second part on another slip of paper. Give the first parts to participants on one side of the room and the second parts to participants on the other side. Have a person from side 1 read theirs and then a person from side 2 read theirs right after it. When they read them to each other, they should be very humorous. Examples:

> The early bird. .is the devil's playground.
> April flowers. . .make the man.
> One rotten apple. . .makes the heart grow fonder.

4. **Intellectual Sayings**. Figure out what these intellectual sayings are in plain language or give a well-known saying and have the participants figure a way of saying it using big words. If you use a large pad on an easel or a blackboard, it will facilitate this. Examples:

Refrain from enumerating your female fowl prior to their emerging from the ovum. (Don't count your chickens before they hatch.)

The passageway to Dante's inferno is macadamized with meritorious resolutions. (The road to hell is paved with good intentions.)

That part of the populace that resides in abodes constructed of transparent substances must refrain from hurling undersized boulders. (People who live in glass houses shouldn't throw stones.)

One's candor in all things is an unequalled strategic plan. (Honesty is the best policy.)

Inaudibility is shining and lustrous. (Silence is golden.)

In the supposition that a conforming leather covering is available for the supporting appendage of one's lower extremity, one must employ its use. (If the shoe fits, wear it.)

Attractiveness can be said to be of no greater depth than the epidermis. (Beauty is only skin deep.)

Tardiness is preferable to a failure to materialize. (Better late than never.)

Refrain from placing the sum total of the products of one's female fowl into a single woven container. (Don't put all your eggs in one basket.)

One's performance communicates over and above one's pronouncements. (Actions speak louder than words.)

5. **Advice Columns**. Have a "Dear Abby," "Ann Landers," or "Miss Manners" group. Clip the advice columns of one of these columnists from the newspaper. Read the question, ask the participants to share what their advice would be, and then read the answer printed in the newspaper. Ask the participants if any of them would like to write an advice column.

DISCUSSION

1. Could some of you share what your favorite sayings are? What was your mother's favorite or most frequently used saying? (Michele Slung has coined a name for mother's advice, "Momilies," and has written a book about it, called *Momilies, As My Mother Used to Say*.)

2. Have any of you ever known someone who used sayings like these all the time? Who was it?

3. Have any of you ever known people who spent all their time giving advice? Did you listen to any of it?

4. Can any of you remember the best advice you ever had? Can you remember the worst?

5. If a young person came to you asking for advice on how to live the best or the happiest life, what would you say?

You may want to end the session by singing one of the advice songs listed at the beginning or you could play a recording of Frank Sinatra singing "Young at Heart." You could also serve Chinese fortune cookies, which are often filled with more advice than fortunes.

IN THE MOOD

Music Possibilities - The more music you include in this session, the more enjoyable it will be.

1. Play original recordings of artists singing popular songs of 1910-1950. The Smithsonian Institution has produced a record collection called "American Popular Song." It's a wonderful resource for this session. Also, Presta Sounds has several appropriate tapes, including "Exercise with Fred Astaire" and "Exercise with Fats Waller." (See Appendix A.) Look for these popular singers in your search for recordings:

Fred Astaire	Tony Bennett
Dick Haymes	Nat "King" Cole
Frank Sinatra	Connie Boswell
Lena Horne	Bessie Smith
Kate Smith	Ethel Waters
Ella Fitzgerald	Helen Morgan
Mel Torme	Margaret Whiting
Judy Garland	Sarah Vaughan
Dinah Shore	Louis Armstrong
Bing Crosby	Helen Forrest
Perry Como	Marlene Dietrich
Billie Holiday	Pearl Bailey

2. Play orchestral collections of popular songs of 1900-1950 (Mantovani Orchestra, The Living Strings, Reader's Digest song collections, Longines Symphony).

3. Have a musician play or sing popular songs, such as those in the Reader's Digest songbook collections. (See Appendix A.)

Visual Possibilities - Old sheet music, books of song collections, old radio microphone (or a picture of one), pictures of famous singers (see list above) and composers such as George Gershwin, Cole Porter, Irving Berlin, Richard Rodgers, Hoagy Carmichael, Jerome Kern, Duke Ellington. Sources for these photographs: Time-Life Books' *This Fabulous Century* (1930-1940 and 1940-1950), *Great Radio Personalities in Historic Photographs* from Vestal Press, and Dover Publication's *Muray's Celebrity Portraits of the Twenties and Thirties.*

ACTIVITIES

1. **Name that Tune**. Play excerpts of songs (without the lyrics) and let the participants guess the name of the song. In a small group, the participants could say the name as they think of it, or you could ask each participant to identify a song in turn. In a large group, try these rules:

> Divide the group into three or four teams.
> Let the teams take turns in guessing the name of a song.
> Each team's members have to agree on one answer.
> If someone guesses out of turn, start over with a new song.
> If a team is stumped, go on to the next team on the same song. If no team knows the name, start all over with a new song.
> Play for a specified length of time, a certain number of rounds, or until one team reaches a certain score.

2. **Photographs**. If you have found several pieces of old sheet music with singers' pictures on them or have old photographs of popular singers, let the participants guess who the performers are. (A young Kate Smith looked very different than in her later years and people will be surprised.) You could also use this as a way of stimulating discussion about the performer. Examples of questions:

> Who is this? What do you remember about him/her?
> Do you remember what songs he/she made famous?
> Did you ever see this person performing?
> Did you listen to him/her on the radio?

3. **Signature songs**. If you can find the recordings, play signature songs (songs for which an artist was particularly known) of popular singers and let the participants guess who it is. If you don't have the recordings, you or a volunteer could either play or sing the song or you could name the song and let the participants name the singer with which it was associated. If your group enjoys singing, you could sing some of the songs together. Examples:

> "When the Moon comes Over the Mountain" or "God Bless America" - **Kate Smith**
> "Where the Blue of the Night Meets the Gold of the Day" or "White Christmas" -
>   **Bing Crosby**
> "Thanks for the Memory" - **Bob Hope**
> "A-Tisket, A-Tasket" - **Ella Fitzgerald**
> "Over the Rainbow" - **Judy Garland**
> "God Bless the Child" - **Billie Holiday**

"I'm Gonna Wash That Man Right Outta My Hair" - **Mary Martin**
"Stormy Weather" - **Lena Horne** or **Ethel Waters**
"I Left My Heart in San Francisco" - **Tony Bennett**
"Catch a Falling Star" - **Perry Como**
"Top Hat" or "Cheek to Cheek" - **Fred Astaire**
"Everything's Coming Up Roses" or "I Got Rhythm" - **Ethel Merman**
"I'll Never Smile Again" or "Strangers in the Night" - **Frank Sinatra**
"Mammy" or "Sonny Boy" - **Al Jolson**
"Vagabond Lover" or "Goodnight, Sweetheart" - **Rudy Vallee**
"In the Mood" or "Don't Sit Under the Apple Tree" - **Andrews Sisters**
"Mona Lisa" or "Unforgettable" - **Nat "King" Cole**
"Rudolph, the Red-Nosed Reindeer" - **Gene Autry**
"Toot Toot Tootsie" - **Eddie Cantor**

4. **Songs Associated With Historical Events**. Name or play the following songs and ask the residents if they remember what historical events are associated with them:

"Yankee Doodle" - **About George Washington in the Revolution**
"Star Spangled Banner" - **War of 1812**
"Clementine" - **1849 Gold Rush**
"John Brown's Body" and "Battle Hymn of the Republic" - **Civil War**
"Meet Me in St. Louis, Louis" - **1904 World's Fair**
"Joe Hill" and "Union Maid" - **Union movement**
"Pack Up Your Troubles in Your Old Kit Bag" (1915) and "Good-bye, Broadway, Hello, France!" (1917) - **World War I**
"Over There" - **World War I** (written by George M. Cohan in 1917 to encourage Americans to sign up for the war)
"How You Gonna Keep 'Em Down on the Farm" (1919) - **Written immediately following World War I, it was about the sophistication of the returning "dough boys"**
"Everyday Will Be Sunday When the Town Goes Dry" (1918) - **Coming of Prohibition**
"Charleston" (1923) - **Dance of the Roaring 20s**
"Lucky Lindy" - **Solo flight of Charles Lindbergh across the Atlantic in 1927**
"Mammy" 1927 - **Sung by Al Jolson in the first full-length movie containing talking and singing, "The Jazz Singer"**
"Happy Days are Here Again" (1929) - **Used as Franklin Roosevelt's campaign song**
"Brother, Can You Spare a Dime," "In a Shanty in Old Shanty Town," and "Who's Afraid of the Big Bad Wolf" - **The Great Depression**
"Tumbling Tumbleweeds" (1934) - **1930s Dust Bowl**

"September Song" (1938) and "The Last Time I Saw Paris" (1940) - **Coming war in Europe**

"The White Cliffs of Dover" (1941) - **England at war**

"Don't Sit Under the Apple Tree" and "This is the Army, Mr. Jones" - **World War II**

5. **Favorites**. Ask the participants, in advance, to tell you one of their favorite songs. You could do three different things with this information. (1) Ask participants to share, in the group, why that song is a favorite. (With what personal event is it associated?) (2) Find recordings of the songs and play them for the group. (3) Sing the songs as a group.

6. **Lyrics Quiz**

   Why is it time to roll out the barrel?   **"For the gang's all here"**

   What am I gonna sit right down and do?   **"Write myself a letter"**

   "Back home again in . . . **Indiana**"

   "It's a sin to . . . **tell a lie**"

   I wore a big red rose and you wore . . . **A bright yellow tulip**

   Nothing could be finer than to be where?   **In "Carolina in the morning"**

   Where did I find a million dollar baby?   **"In a 5 and 10 cent store"**

   Who am I just wild about?   **Harry**

   Who is coming away with me "in my merry oldsmobile"?   **Lucile**

   When will we dance the hootchie-kootchie?   **"If you will meet me in St. Louis, Louis"**

   What will you wear on your golden wedding day?   **An "old grey bonnet"**

   What did I wear "til it wilted"?   **"My sweet little Alice Blue Gown"**

   For whom are the bells ringing?   **"For me and my gal"**

   When should you look for the silver lining?   **"Whene'er a cloud appears in the blue"**

   When is many a heart aching?   **"After the ball"**

   What is a grand old name?   **Mary**

   What is taught to the tune of a hickory stick?   **"Readin' and writin' and 'rithmetic"**

   When you were my "queen in calico," what was I?   **"Your bashful, barefoot beau"**

   When we get to the preacher, what will I say?   **"Yes sir, that's my baby"**

   What is the "best band in the land"?   **Alexander's Ragtime Band**

7. **Related Activity**. Show a movie musical from the 1930s or 1940s, such as one of these:

   • Judy Garland films - "Meet Me in St. Louis," "Easter Parade"
   • "Oklahoma"
   • Fred Astaire/Ginger Rogers films - "Top Hat," "The Gay Divorcee," "Swing Time"
   • Gene Kelly films - "An American in Paris," "Singin' in the Rain"
   • "Showboat"
   • "Pennies from Heaven" (Bing Crosby version)
   • "Rose-Marie" or "Naughty Marietta"
   • "Til the Clouds Roll By" (biography of Jerome Kern)

8. **Related Activity**. Listen to some old musical-variety radio shows, such as those by Eddie Cantor, Bing Crosby, Kate Smith.

DISCUSSION

1. Can some of you share your earliest memories of singing songs? Did any of you ever sing in school? Do you remember what you sang?

2. In the years before radio was widespread, where did you hear new songs? (vaudeville houses, theaters, dances, band concerts, music boxes, gramophone, player piano, song pluggers in music stores?)

3. Do any of you have a favorite composer of songs? If so, do you remember what songs he or she wrote? (See the Addendum on the next page for famous composers and some of their songs.)

4. Who were your favorite singers? Did you ever see any "in person" at local theaters or vaudeville houses? Did you hear them on the radio?

5. Did any of you ever sing for groups or on the stage? Tell us about it.

6. Can any of you think of a song that had particular meaning for you in your life, positive or negative? Could you tell us about it? (You might ask this question earlier and give them a little time to think about it.)

7. Did any of you ever remember singing songs in the movie theater with the words flashed on the screen? ("song slides")

You could end the session by singing a favorite popular song, like "God Bless America" or "Let Me Call You Sweetheart."

Addendum

Here are some of the most popular composers of the 1920s, 1930s, and 1940s and some of their songs:

Irving Berlin - "God Bless America," "I Love a Piano," "Alexander's Ragtime Band," "Puttin' On the Ritz," "Isn't This a Lovely Day," "Cheek To Cheek," "Always," "They Say It's Wonderful," "What'll I Do?"

Cole Porter - "Night and Day," "You're the Top," "What Is This Thing Called Love?" "I've Got You Under My Skin," "Just One Of Those Things," "I Get a Kick Out Of You"

Rodgers and Hart - "It Never Entered My Mind," "You Are Too Beautiful," "Little Girl Blue," "Dancing On the Ceiling," "This Can't Be Love," "Glad To Be Unhappy," "My Funny Valentine"

George Gershwin - "The Man I Love," "Fascinating Rhythm," "They Can't Take That Away From Me," "Embraceable You," "But Not For Me," "Our Love Is Here To Stay," "'S Wonderful," "Nice Work If You Can Get It," "I Got Rhythm"

Hoagy Carmichael - "Georgia On My Mind," "Skylark," "The Nearness Of You," "Star Dust," "Up a Lazy River"

Duke Ellington - "Sophisticated Lady," "Satin Doll," "Take the 'A' Train," "It Don't Mean a Thing," "I Got It Bad (And That Ain't Good)," "Mood Indigo"

Harold Arlen - "Come Rain Or Come Shine," "My Shining Hour," "Last Night When We Were Young," "Blues In the Night," "The Man That Got Away," "Get Happy," "Stormy Weather," "Ac-cent-tchu-ate the Positive"

Jerome Kern - "All the Things You Are," "Can't Stop Lovin' That Man," "Ol' Man River," "Why Do I Love You," "Make Believe"

Rodgers and Hammerstein - "Hello, Young Lovers," "Oklahoma," "Oh, What a Beautiful Mornin'," "It's a Grand Night For Singing," "It Might As Well Be Spring," "Some Enchanted Evening," "You'll Never Walk Alone"

IN THE MOOD

Music Possibilities - Recordings of original big band music. Some good sources are your local library, Presta Sounds, or Publishers Central Bureau. (See Appendix A.) The following are the names of some well-known bandleaders of 1920-1950: Glenn Miller, Tommy Dorsey, Benny Goodman, Artie Shaw, Harry James, Charlie Barnet, Les Brown, Duke Ellington, Jimmy Dorsey, Bob Crosby, Louis Armstrong, Chick Webb, Guy Lombardo, Kay Kyser, Paul Whiteman, Vaughn Monroe, Ray Noble, Count Basie, King Oliver, Fletcher Henderson, and Jelly Roll Morton. Note: Among the best song collections and books written about the big band era are by George Simon.

Visual Possibilities - Sheet music and record album covers of big band music; musical instruments or pictures of them (saxophone, trumpet, drums, clarinet, trombone); pictures of big bands, singers, and bandleaders. (See *This Fabulous Century*, 1930-1940 and 1940-1950.)

ACTIVITIES

1. **Big Band Songs.** Have a singer perform, or play a tape of, some well-known songs made popular by big bands. Here are some suggestions, with the vocalists who made them famous:

   "A-Tisket, A-Tasket" - Ella Fitzgerald
   "I Don't Want To Walk Without You" - Helen Forrest
   "I'll Never Smile Again" - Frank Sinatra
   "Minnie the Moocher" - Cab Calloway
   "Oh, Johnny, Oh Johnny, Oh!" - "Wee" Bonnie Baker
   "Sentimental Journey" - Doris Day
   "There! I've Said It Again" - Vaughn Monroe
   "Willow Weep For Me" - Mildred Bailey

"And the Angels Sing" - "Liltin'" Martha Tilton
"I've Heard That Song Before" - Helen Forrest
"One For My Baby" - Fred Astaire
"Ain't Misbehavin'" - Fats Waller
"Basin Street Blues" - Jack Teagarden
"Boo-hoo" - Carmen Lombardo
"Chattanooga Choo Choo" - Marion Hutton and Tex Beneke
"Deep Purple" - Bea Wain
"Don't Sit Under the Apple Tree" - Andrews Sisters
"Goody, Goody" - Helen Ward
"Got a Date With an Angel" - Skinney Ennis
"I'm Glad There is You" - Bob Eberly
"I'm Gonna Sit Right Down and Write Myself a Letter" - Fats Waller
"Laura" - Woody Herman
"Nighty-Night" - The King Sisters

If some of the participants were born in the 1920s or later, they might be able to match some of the songs with their titles and with the singers. People born before that will probably find the music familiar but will not remember specifics. You could ask them what they do remember about each song or if the song has any special meaning to anyone. Ask them, too, if there are any other songs from this era that they particularly like or remember.

2. **Pictures**. If you can find pictures of well-known personalities of the big band era, show them to the participants and see if they can identify the person and tell what they remember about them. (Try to use pictures that were taken in the 1920s, 1930s, and 1940s.) If you don't have pictures, you could ask the participants what they remember about the early careers of the following people:

Andrews Sisters (Maxene, Patti, Laverne)	Billie Holiday
Bing Crosby	Bob Eberly
Lawrence Welk	Fats Waller
Ella Fitzgerald	Louis Armstrong
Guy Lombardo	Doris Day
Lena Horne	Rudy Vallee
Duke Ellington	Dinah Shore
Frank Sinatra	Cab Calloway
Mel Torme	Peggy Lee
Perry Como	

3. **Instruments**. What instruments did these bandleaders play:

Glenn Miller - **Trombone**	Eddy Duchin - **Piano**
Guy Lombardo - **Violin**	Tommy Dorsey - **Trombone**
Benny Goodman - **Clarinet**	Jimmy Dorsey - **Saxophone, Clarinet**
Harry James - **Trumpet**	Alvino Rey - **Guitar**
Duke Ellington - **Piano**	Vaughn Monroe - **Trumpet**
Chick Webb - **Drums**	Artie Shaw - **Clarinet**
Gene Krupa - **Drums**	Count Basie - **Piano**

4. **Big Band Trivia**.

> Whose younger brother was bandleader Bob Crosby? **Bing Crosby**
>
> What other brothers worked together? **Jimmy and Tommy Dorsey, Guy and Carmen Lombardo**
>
> Who was known as "The Waltz King"? **Wayne King**
>
> What bandleader was killed in World War II? **Glenn Miller**
>
> Who was known as "The Sentimental Gentleman of Swing"? **Tommy Dorsey**
>
> What big bandleader married Betty Grable? **Harry James**
>
> With what band did the Modernaires sing? **Glenn Miller band**
>
> Who was called the "King of Jazz," leading the first big band in the 1920s? **Paul "Pops" Whiteman**
>
> Who hosted the radio quiz show "Kollege of Musical Knowledge"? **Kay Kyser**
>
> Who hosted the first radio variety show, "The Fleischman Hour"? **Rudy Vallee, with the "Connecticut Yankees"**
>
> What were *Downbeat* and *Metronome*? **Trade magazines of the big band musicians**

5. **Theme Songs**. Play theme songs of the big bands and let the participants guess which band played it. (If you don't have recordings, it may be difficult for the participants to identify most of these since they knew them by sound and not by name.)

> "Summertime" - **Bob Crosby**
> "When It's Sleepy Time Down South" - **Louis Armstrong**
> "Sentimental Journey" - **Les Brown**
> "Minnie the Moocher" - **Cab Calloway**
> "I'm Getting Sentimental Over You" - **Tommy Dorsey**
> "Take the 'A' Train" or "Satin Doll" - **Duke Ellington**
> "Let's Dance" - **Benny Goodman**
> "Ciribiribin" - **Harry James**
> "The Waltz You Saved for Me" - **Wayne King**
> "Auld Lang Syne" - **Guy Lombardo**
> "Moonlight Serenade" - **Glenn Miller**
> "Sleep" - **Fred Waring**
> "Bubbles in the Wine" - **Lawrence Welk**
> "Rhapsody in Blue" - **Paul Whiteman**

6. **Today's Big Band Music**. If you are able to find recordings, play some more contemporary versions of some big band songs. . .a disco version or one from a synthesizer. Several present-day pop singers have recorded songs made popular in the 1930s and 1940s (e.g., Judy Collins and Linda Ronstadt). It would be interesting to play a song or two for comparison. Ask the participants which they prefer.

7. **Big Bands Today**. Big bands are making a comeback. If there is a local radio station that plays music of the 1930s and 1940s, tell the residents what it is. Bring in any newspaper articles or ads you can find about local big band dances.

8. **Slang**. Ask the participants if they know what these slang terms mean:

>Disc or platter - **a record**
>Long hair - **someone who prefers symphonic music to swing**
>Canary - **female vocalist**
>Cutting the rug - **dancing to swing music**
>Jitterbug - **someone dancing to swing music**
>Licorice stick - **clarinet**
>88 or Mothbox - **piano**
>One-nighter - **a one-night playing engagement**
>Schmaltz - **sweet, sentimental music**
>Truckin' - **a finger-waving, hip-tossing walk**

9. **Related Activity**. Show one of these feature films about big bands: "The Glenn Miller Story," "The Eddy Duchin Story," "The Big Broadcast of 1937," "Let's Make Music," "The Benny Goodman Story," "Second Chorus," "Stagedoor Canteen," "The Fabulous Dorseys," "Private Buckaroo."

10. **Related Activity**. Plan an evening dance for the participants, inviting families and friends to come, too. (You might be able to find a few extra men to dance by contacting a local senior center.) You could call the evening a "Make Believe Ballroom" and even rent a revolving mirrored ball for the ceiling.

Here are some sources for bands: (1) Some senior centers have bands formed by retired people. (2) A local band might be willing to come to your facility on their rehearsal night. (3) Contact your local Lions or Kiwanis Club (or any other service groups) to see if they can find a band for you.

This can be an excellent public relations tool for the facility, particularly if you make a special effort to get family members to attend. (Send a special invitation or put an invitation in with the monthly billing.) Your administrator might be willing to provide money, outside your budget, to pay the expenses. Try to get newspaper or television coverage. At the very least, you could send a press release. After the event, you could write an article and send a good picture to the newspapers..."Local nursing home recreates 'The Make Believe Ballroom.'" The more staff support you have (starting with the Administrator, the Director of Nursing, and the Food Service Manager), the easier it will be.

DISCUSSION

1. Do any of you remember what you thought about the swinging big band music when you first heard it? Did any of you prefer the sweet band music, like Guy Lombardo's, to swing?

2. Did any of you like to go out dancing in your middle years? Where did you go? What kind of music was your favorite for dancing?

3. Did any of you listen to big band programs on the radio, such as "Coca-Cola Spotlight Bands" or "Make Believe Ballroom"? Do you remember any other music programs you liked or preferred?

4. Did any of you have children who were "jitterbugs"? What did you think of that?

5. What kind of music do you prefer hearing today?

IN THE MOOD

Music Possibilities

1. Play the soundtrack of a Broadway musical from 1927-1950. Suggestions: "Showboat," "Annie Get Your Gun," "Guys and Dolls," "The Boys from Syracuse," "Pal Joey," "Kiss Me Kate," "On the Town," "Oklahoma," "Carousel," "South Pacific," "The King and I," "Finian's Rainbow," "Porgy and Bess," "Call Me Madam," "Girl Crazy," "Oh, Kay!" "Funny Face," "On Your Toes," "Bloomer Girl."

2. Play a recording of a collection of Broadway songs. Check your library to try to find one with the original artists or of an original star singing Broadway songs, such as Mary Martin, Ethel Merman, John Raitt, Paul Robeson, Ethel Waters, Howard Keel, Dorothy Kirsten, Helen Morgan, Alfred Drake.

3. If you have a pianist or other soloist, play songs from Broadway shows.

4. Songs about Broadway:

   "Goodbye, Broadway, Hello, France!" (1917)
   "Lullaby of Broadway" (From "42nd Street")
   "Let Me Entertain You" (From "Gypsy")
   "No Business Like Show Business" (From "Annie Get Your Gun")
   "We Open in Venice" and "Another Op-ning, Another Show" (From "Kiss Me, Kate")

Visual Possibilities

1. Album covers of soundtracks of Broadway shows.

2. Make posters with the names of Broadway musicals on them and post in the activity room.

Down Memory Lane

3. Photographs of composers and performers associated with the early Broadway musical stage or photographs or scenes from the plays themselves. (Dover Publications' *Great Actors and Actresses of the American Stage* covers 1940 and after.) Some performers are listed earlier. Composers: George and Ira Gershwin, Jerome Kern, Irving Berlin, Oscar Hammerstein, Richard Rodgers, Harold Arlen, Frank Loesser, Kurt Weill, Eubie Blake, George M. Cohan.

ACTIVITIES

1. **Associations**. Name the following objects, or show pictures of them, and ask the participants if they know with which show each could be associated:

>Merry-go-round - **"Carousel"**
>Horse and buggy, cowboy hat - **"Oklahoma"**
>Steamboat - **"Showboat"**
>Ballet slippers - **"On Your Toes"**
>Dice - **"Guys and Dolls"**
>Sailor - **"On the Town"** or **"South Pacific"**
>Oriental children - **"South Pacific"** or **"The King and I"**

2. **Broadway Songs**. Play excerpts of Broadway songs (or name the songs) and ask the participants if they remember the song and from which musical it came. Play the songs live or use recordings. There are many collections of Broadway songs available in libraries and music stores. Examples:

>"How are Things in Glocca Morra?" - **"Finian's Rainbow"**
>"Surrey with the Fringe on Top" - **"Oklahoma"**
>"Summertime" - **"Porgy and Bess"** (also considered an opera)
>"Bali Ha'i" - **"South Pacific"**
>"76 Trombones" - **"The Music Man"**
>"Anything You Can Do I Can Do Better" - **"Annie Get Your Gun"**
>"Ol' Man River" - **"Showboat"**
>"New York, New York" - **"On the Town"**
>"Shall We Dance" - **"The King and I"**
>"You'll Never Walk Alone" - **"Carousel"**

3. **Personalities**. If you have found pictures of Broadway stars and composers, pass them around and see if the participants can identify the people and/or can share their memories of ever seeing any of these people. (Look for books about Broadway musicals, as well as books about specific composers or performers.)

4. **Current Shows**. Share with the participants what musicals are currently hits on Broadway or on national tour, as well as any revivals of older plays. Briefly tell the basic plot, play some music excerpts, share any pictures you have. The soundtrack albums will have most of this information. ("Chorus Line," "Cats," and "Sweeney Todd" should be available in the library.) Encourage the participants to share in a discussion of how plays today are different from the golden age of the Broadway musical, including plot, music, and cost.

5. **Reading Plays**. If your group likes to read plays, prepare a scene from one of their favorites in largeprint and have your group read through it. (Scripts of plays can be found in the library.) You could play the songs from the soundtrack at appropriate times or just read the words to the songs.

6. **Plots**. Give the plots of the following musicals and let the participants guess what the play is:

> A man and a woman have a contest to see who can shoot the best and later they fall in love.
> **"Annie Get Your Gun"**

> A young woman falls in love with a gambler, who later leaves her but returns in time for the finale.
> **"Showboat"**

> The play "The Taming of the Shrew" is taking place on the stage while the two stars from that play are fighting off the stage.
> **"Kiss Me, Kate"**

> A Frenchman falls in love with a young American woman on an island.
> **"South Pacific"**

> Three sailors are in search of women and fun in New York City.
> **"On the Town"**

> An Englishwoman becomes a teacher in Siam.
> **"The King and I"**

> A young woman falls in love with a barker in an amusement park.
> **"Carousel"**

> A boy falls in love with a girl who is only awake one day every 100 years.
> **"Brigadoon"**

> A young woman goes to a box social with the wrong man in a horse and buggy, but later marries the one she really loves.
> **"Oklahoma"**

7. **Related Activity**. Most high schools put on a play each year, oftentimes a musical. Ask your local school to come to your facility and perform some scenes for the participants. Some of the participants might like to go to the school to see the play.

8. **Related Activity**. Show a movie that is based on a Broadway musical. Suggestions: "South Pacific," "Carousel," "Oklahoma," "Gay Divorcee," "Pal Joey," "Showboat," "Funny Face," "Annie Get Your Gun," "The King and I," "On the Town."

9. **Related Activity**. If your group likes drama and is very active, you could act out a play in condensed form. Here is what Fahrney-Keedy Memorial Home in Boonsboro, Maryland, did successfully, even taking it "on the road":

The administrator, a former activities director, got the script and the soundtrack to "Hello, Dolly," a play which takes place at the turn of the century. The plot was condensed to the essential scenes and dialogue (about 45 minutes altogether). The dialogue was prerecorded with the soundtrack music added at appropriate times. After the tape was made, residents were chosen to play each part and they rehearsed a pantomime of each scene. Scenery, lighting, and costumes were added, primarily by staff members from every department. The highlight of the show was when "Hello, Dolly" was sung and the 90-year old "Dolly" came off the stage to sit in the laps of men in the audience.

DISCUSSION

1. What musicals are your favorites? What musicals have any of you seen on the stage? What do you remember about them?

2. Have any of you ever seen a play on Broadway? Do you remember who the stars were? Tell us about it.

3. What musicals have any of you seen in the movies? Which was better, the play or the movie?

4. Have any of you ever been a part of the production of a play or a musical? Tell us about it.

IN THE MOOD

Music Possibilities

1. Recording of Saint-Saens' "Carnival of the Animals" or Prokofiev's "Peter and the Wolf."

2. Recording of songs known to children at the turn of the century. (Look for children's records at your local library.) Examples:

"Comin' Round the Mountain"	"Skip to my Lou"
"Jim Crack Corn"	"Rock-a-bye Baby"
"I Had a Rooster"	"Home on the Range"
"I've Been Workin' on the Railroad"	"Three Blind Mice"
"My Bonnie"	"Mulberry Bush"
"America"	"Baa, Baa, Black Sheep"
"Oh Susanna"	"Lavender's Blue"
"Polly Wolly Doodle"	"Ding Dong Bell"
"Old Gray Mare"	"Old King Cole"

3. Songs about children and toys:

"Baby Face"	"You Must Have Been a Beautiful Baby"
"Babes in Arms"	"Kids!" (From "Bye Bye Birdie")
"Parade of the Wooden Soldiers"	"Rockabye Your Baby with a Dixie Melody"
"Toyland"	"Little Man, You've Had A Busy Day"
"Santa Claus is Comin' to Town"	"Pretty Baby"

Down Memory Lane

Visual Possibilities

1. Pictures or a display of toys such as these: kite, yo-yo, marbles, jacks, baseball, football, jump rope, stilts, comic books, harmonica, roller skates (the kind that fit on your shoes with a key), croquet, piggy bank, rag doll, china doll, small hobby horse, Davy Crockett hat, tea set, tricycle, wooden train set.

2. Old children's books, such as these: *Peter Rabbit, Mother Goose, Aesop's Fables, Alice in Wonderland, Wizard of Oz*, Kipling's *Jungle Book, Winnie the Pooh.*

3. Pictures of children from 1890-1910. (Check old Sears or Wards catalogs or "Good Old Days" magazines.)

4. Sayings written on large posters: "Like father, like son"; "Spare the rod and spoil the child"; "Children should be seen and not heard"; "The Child is Father to the Man"; "Out of the mouths of babes often come gems."

ACTIVITIES

1. **Children**. This would be a good program for inviting participants' grandchildren and/or great-grandchildren to come and share. They can answer many of the quiz questions and maybe sing for, or with, the group. You could invite the children to bring in their favorite toy to share and then ask each participant if she/he remembers a favorite toy.

2. **Toys**. If you've been able to find any objects having to do with childhood (as listed under Visual Possibilities), share them with the participants. Ask the participants and their families if they have any original ones that you could borrow. Check antique stores (maybe you can borrow some objects), flea markets, used book stores, or estate sales.

3. **Games**. Talk about universal games of childhood. Give the name of the game and have the participants tell how to play. Or describe the game and let the participants guess the name of the game. Ask the group which games they played the most or liked the best. Ask if there are any other games that they played besides these. If there are children there, ask them what their favorite games are.

leapfrog	jacks
jump rope	Simon says
stilts	red rover
mumbletypeg	ring around the rosy
croquet	London Bridge
hopscotch	roller skating
baseball	Mother, may I
hide and seek	run, sheepie, run
marbles	follow the leader
roll the hoop	king of the mountain
yo-yo	red light, green light
tug of war	collecting lightning bugs

4. **Nursery Rhymes.** Give the first line of short nursery rhymes and ask individual participants to finish them. Ask them if they remember who taught them these nursery rhymes and if they taught them to their own children and grandchildren.

  Jack be nimble, Jack be quick. . .
  Patty cake, patty cake. . .
  Hey diddle, diddle, the cat and the fiddle. . .
  Little Jack Horner sat in a corner. . .
  Humpty Dumpty sat on a wall. . .
  Jack and Jill went up the hill. . .
  Old Mother Hubbard went to her cupboard. . .
  Little Bo Peep has lost her sheep. . .
  Mary, Mary, quite contrary. . .
  Hickory, dickory dock. . .
  Little Miss Muffet. . .
  Georgie Porgie. . .
  Sing a song of sixpence. . .
  Little boy blue, come blow your horn. . .
  Twinkle, twinkle, little star. . .
  Baa, baa, black sheep. . .
  Three blind mice. . .

5. **Singing Games.** Have the participants describe and/or sing these singing games: London Bridge, Ring around a-rosie, Hokey-pokey. You might have some children come in and chant some jump rope rhymes while they jump rope.

6. **Dolls.** There are many doll collectors and some cities have doll repair shops, dollhouse museums, or antique shops that specialize in dolls. Invite one of these collectors to share their vintage dolls and to talk about their history and how they obtained the dolls. Ask the participants beforehand if any of their dolls are still in the family and if they would share them. You might also bring in a couple of the latest dolls on the market, such as Barbie, Strawberry Shortcake, or Cabbage Patch dolls.

7. **Stories.** You can give the basic plot or describe the characters of a fairy tale or children's story and let the participants guess the name of the story. Suggestions:

Chicken Little	Alice in Wonderland
Princess and the Pea	Snow White
Winnie the Pooh	Jack and the Beanstalk
Gingerbread Man	Hansel and Gretel
Mary Poppins	Emperor's New Clothes
Pinocchio	Beauty and the Beast
Wizard of Oz	Cinderella
The Ugly Duckling	Little Red Riding Hood
Peter Rabbit	The Three Bears
Rapunzel	Three Little Pigs

8. **Halloween**. If you were to do this in conjunction with Halloween, you could invite some of the grandchildren and staff children to come in and show off their Halloween costumes. The participants and children could talk about Halloweens past.

9. **Related Activity**. Show an Andy Hardy movie (starring Mickey Rooney) or a Shirley Temple film ("Captain January," "Little Miss Marker," "Just Around the Corner," "Rebecca of Sunnybrook Farm").

DISCUSSION

1. Do any of you remember learning to whistle? Can you still whistle? Do any of you remember going for hay rides? Can you remember taffypulls? Where could you get penny candy?

2. Do any of the men remember your first hair cut? What were barber shops like? Do you ladies remember how you wore your long hair?

3. Did any of you help with a family business while a child? What did you do?

4. Do any of you remember what chores you had to do around the house? Did any of you get an allowance or money for doing chores? Do you remember how much it was? Do you remember how you usually spent it? Did any of you have a piggy bank? Did you ever save all your money for something very special?

5. How did little boys dress...were knickers or short pants worn? Do any of you men remember when you first wore long pants? How did little girls dress? Did you ever wear bloomers or shorts? Did any of you wear hand-me-downs? Whose were they?

6. Do any of you remember how you celebrated your birthday when growing up? Did any of you ever have a party for your birthday?

7. Was going to church or to synagogue an important part of growing up? Were there things you weren't allowed to do on the Sabbath?

8. Do any of you remember how you were usually disciplined?

9. Is it easier growing up today or 80 years ago?

10. Does anyone have a particularly vivid or happy memory of your childhood that you would like to share?

You might end the session by singing "Down By the Old Mill Stream" and giving out some old-fashioned candy, such as licorice, gumdrops, or peppermint sticks.

IN THE MOOD

Music Possibilities

1. Play comedians' theme songs:

    Bob Hope - "Thanks for the Memory"
    Milton Berle - "Near You"
    Johnny Carson - "The Tonight Show Theme"
    Jimmy Durante - "Inka-Dinka-Doo" or "One of Those Songs"
    Eddie Cantor - "Ida" or "One Hour With You"
    "Amos 'n Andy" radio show - "The Perfect Song"
    "Honeymooners" TV show - "Tenderly"
    Steve Allen - "This Could Be the Start of Something Big"
    "The Aldrich Family" radio show - "This Is It"
    Three Stooges - "Three Blind Mice"
    Jack Benny - "Love in Bloom"
    Groucho Marx - "You Bet Your Life" theme song

2. Play a vintage comedy radio show, such as Jack Benny, "Lum and Abner," "Fibber McGee and Molly," Fred Allen, Abbott and Costello, "Baby Snooks" (Fanny Brice), Burns and Allen.

3. Songs about smiling:

    "Let a Smile Be Your Umbrella"   "Smile"
    "When You're Smiling"   "Smiles"
    "Make 'em Laugh" from "Singin' in the Rain"

28 *Down Memory Lane*

4. Humorous Songs:

"Ma! He's Makin' Eyes at Me"
"Yes! We Have No Bananas"
"It Ain't Necessarily So"
"Button Up Your Overcoat"
"Flat Foot Floogie"
"Mairsy Doats"
"I Cain't Say No" from "Oklahoma"

"K-K-K-Katy"
"You're the Top"
"Swinging on a Star"
"Crazy Words Crazy Tune"
"Three Little Fishies"
"Jeepers Creepers"

Visual Possibilities

1. Pictures of comedians of the past - early TV, movies, radio, and vaudeville stars...any of those listed above, plus these: Beatrice Lillie, Bert Lahr, W.C. Fields, Marx Brothers, Ed Wynn, Sid Caesar, Charlie Chaplin, Danny Kaye, Harold Lloyd, Lucille Ball, Will Rogers, Joe Penner, Ish Kabibble. (There are good pictures in Vestal Press' *Great Radio Personalities in Historic Photographs*.)

2. Make a poster with the comedy and tragedy masks on it and this saying, "Laugh and the world laughs with you, cry and you cry alone."

3. Put posters on the walls with old jokes on them or write a joke on pieces of paper in large, bold print and give to each participant. These are easily found in the juvenile book section of your library. Here are some examples:

Why did the chicken cross the road? **To get to the other side**

"Waiter, what's that fly doing in my soup?" **Waiter: "Looks like the backstroke to me, sir."**

What word is always pronounced wrong? **Wrong**

Can you name the capital of every state in the United States in 10 seconds? **Washington, D.C.**

How much dirt is in a hole two-feet by one-foot by two-feet? **None**

If you were to throw a white stone into the Red Sea, what would it become? **Wet**

What do you take off last before you go to bed? **You take your feet off the floor**

What always has one eye open but cannot see? **A needle**

ACTIVITIES

1. **Favorites**. Ask the participants to name their favorite comedians. If you have pictures, pass them around and let the participants guess who they are. Ask them to share some memories of each comedian.

2. **Jokes**. In advance, ask the participants to come to the activity with a joke to tell. You could use them all at once or spread them throughout the activity. Before the session starts, you might go around the group to find out who has a joke to tell to the group. NOTE: If you can record the jokes that participants bring, either on tape or on paper, you could use them in your facility newsletter, giving recognition to the teller.

3. **Comedy Partners.** Give one partner's name and ask the participants to name the other.

Dean Martin...**Jerry Lewis**	Bob...**Ray**
George Burns...**Gracie Allen**	Edgar Bergen...**Charlie McCarthy**
Abbott...**Costello**	Jack Benny...**Mary Livingston or Rochester**
Fibber McGee...**Molly**	Paul Winchell...**Jerry Mahoney**
Lum...**Abner**	Lucille Ball...**Desi Arnaz**
Amos...**Andy**	Fred Mertz...**Ethel**
Bob Hope...**Bing Crosby**	Sid Caesar...**Imogene Coca**
Ozzie Nelson...**Harriet**	Stan Laurel...**Oliver Hardy**

4. **Quotations.** Say the following quotes and have the participants guess which comedian said it.

"This is another fine mess you've gotten me into." **Oliver Hardy to Stan Laurel**

"Heeere's Johnny!" **Ed McMahan introducing Johnny Carson**

"Oh, Rochester!" **Jack Benny**

"Hey, Abbbbbbott!" **Lou Costello**

"That's a joke, son." **Senator Claghorn on Fred Allen's radio show**

"Everybody wants to get into de act." **Jimmy Durante**

"How sweet it is." **Jackie Gleason**

"Well, I'll be a dirty bird." **George Gobel**

"Wanna buy a duck?" **Joe Penner**

"What a revoltin' development this is." **Chester Riley (William Bendix) in "The Life of Riley"**

"Beulah, peel me a grape." **Mae West**

"Now cut that out!" **Jack Benny**

"I got a million of 'em" **Jimmy Durante**

"Gotta straighten out that closet one of these days." **Fibber McGee**

5. **Secret Word.** Have a secret word (or more) that an assistant knows. If a participant says it, have the assistant ring a bell and give a prize to that participant, as on Groucho Marx's "You Bet Your Life." (It would be even more authentic if you have the prize in the mouth of a stuffed duck.)

6. **Comedians' Trivia.**

Who was known as "The Little Tramp"? **Charlie Chaplin**

Who used the famous routine called "Who's On First"? **Abbott and Costello**

Who was known as "The Schnoz"? **Jimmy Durante**

Who had an eternally over-stuffed closet? **Fibber McGee**

Who was known as "Mr. Television"? **Milton Berle**

Who were the stars of television's "Your Show of Shows"? **Sid Caesar and Imogene Coca**

Who made the "road" pictures? **Bob Hope and Bing Crosby**

Who was the first host of "The Tonight Show"? **Steve Allen**

On whose radio show was Allen's Alley? **Fred Allen**

Which comedian had a car that was a broken-down Maxwell? **Jack Benny**

Which Marx brother never spoke? **Harpo**

Which Marx brother had the big mustache? **Groucho**

Which Marx brother used the Italian accent? **Chico**

Who played Baby Snooks? **Fanny Brice**

What team consisted of a madcap redhead and a crazy Cuban? **Lucille Ball and Desi Arnaz**

Who was Jack Benny's "sidekick"? **Eddie Rochester**

Who was known as "ski nose"? **Bob Hope**

What silent movie comic was known as "Great Stone Face"? **Buster Keaton**

7. **Humor Today**. Tell the participants about current sources of humor that are available locally. "Dial-a-Joke," comedy clubs, comedy radio stations, comedy movies, videotaped comedy acts (such as Richard Pryor or Steve Martin). Share with them comic strips in the local paper, current bestsellers in humor, humorous columns in the paper. Share with them who *your* favorite current comedian is and why. You could read a comic strip you especially like, a short excerpt from a book, or tell a favorite joke. CAUTION: Women in this age group are easily offended by off-color jokes or jokes using profanity, especially when told in mixed company. Gauge your group carefully.

8. **Related Activity**. Show silent films of famous comics, such as Laurel and Hardy, Charlie Chaplin, Harold Lloyd, and Buster Keaton. Show feature-length films that showcased famous comedians, such as Marx Brothers films ("Duck Soup," "Animal Crackers," "The Cocoanuts," "A Night At the Opera," "A Day At the Races"); Abbott and Costello films; "The Road to Rio" and other Hope/Crosby Road pictures; Jack Benny in "Charley's Aunt"; "Damsel in Distress" with Burns and Allen; or a Laurel and Hardy film such as, "The Piano."

DISCUSSION

1. Have any of you seen any famous comedians in person? Tell us about it.

2. Can some of you tell us about the funniest person you ever knew personally?

3. Do any of you remember what comedy was like on vaudeville? Please share it with us.

4. Can some of you share what you think was the funniest radio show?

5. Do any of you remember seeing some humorous plays? What were they? What are some of the funniest movies you have seen?

To end this session, in particular, be sure to "leave 'em laughing" with a joke!

DANCING

IN THE MOOD

Music Possibilities

1. Recording of dance music of the 1920s or 1930s. Check your library or Presta Sounds. (See Appendix A.)

2. Recordings or live music (piano, accordion, organ) using songs written about dancing, such as the following:

"Dancing in the Dark"	"Charleston"
"10 Cents a Dance"	"Shall We Dance"
"Sleepytime Gal"	"Begin the Beguine"
"Dancing on the Ceiling"	"The Band Played On"
"Polka Dots and Moonbeams"	"Ballin' the Jack"
"Skip to My Lou"	"Jersey Bounce"
"After the Ball"	"Hokey-Pokey"
"Meet Me in St. Louis"	"The Continental"
"Stompin' at the Savoy"	"42nd Street"
"I Could Have Danced All Night"	"Waltzing Matilda"
"The Waltz You Saved for Me"	"Cheek to Cheek"
"Let's Face the Music and Dance"	

2. Ragtime music (Scott Joplin). Look for records by Max Morath or the New Orleans Ragtime Orchestra.

3. If you have a group that likes classical dance, play famous ballet music, such as Tchaikovsky's "The Nutcracker" or "Swan Lake."

Visual Possibilities

1. Pictures of famous dancers, such as Fred Astaire, Adele Astaire, Ginger Rogers, Vernon and Irene Castle, Cyd Charisse, Gene Kelly, Agnes de Mille, Martha Graham, Arthur and Kathryn Murray, Shirley Temple, Bill "Bojangles" Robinson.

2. Pictures of couples doing specific dance steps. Look in the library for a book about how to do ballroom dances.

3. Dancers' equipment: toe shoes, tap shoes, top hat, cane.

ACTIVITIES

1. **Dance Demonstration**. Contact a local ballroom teacher and arrange for a demonstration of dance steps of the 1920s, 1930s, and 1940s. (Look for a dance teacher through your local community college and senior centers, as well as dance studios.) Doing the dances in historical order would be the most interesting. If you don't have a demonstration but have found pictures of people dancing, show these and ask the participants if they know what the dances are. You also might have a spry participant couple who could demonstrate. After each dance, ask the participants if they remember these particular dances and if they ever did any of them. Ask them to share memories. Dance suggestions:

Waltz	Fox Trot	Two-step
Charleston	Cakewalk	Shimmy
Hootchy-kootchy	Rumba	Bunny Hug
The Continental	Castle Walk	Lindy Hop
Walkin' the Dog	Big Apple	

2. **Dance Trivia**. As the participants answer these questions, encourage them to talk about their own experiences.

What was the Cake Walk?
A dance contest in which couples strutted around a large circle in high steps. The winning couple got a cake. It was originally done to ragtime music.

What were Tango Teas?
Afternoon affairs held in department stores that combined dancing and a fashion show

Who invented the Castle Walk?
Irene and Vernon Castle

Was the Fox Trot a waltz or a two-step?
A two-step

What was "button shining"?
A 1920s term for when a couple danced very close together

What dance of the 1920s could be described as "knock-kneed and heel-kicking"?
The Charleston

What were marathon dances?
Couples were challenged to see which of them could dance for the most hours

Who was the most famous dance team of the 1930s?
Fred Astaire and Ginger Rogers

Who were jitterbugs?
Young people who danced the Lindy Hop to the swing music of the big bands.

Who were "taxi dancers"?
Young women who would dance with paying customers in dance halls, usually for "Ten Cents a Dance"

What was the dance called "The Big Apple"?
Dancers got in a circle and a leader called out the different dances they were to do

What was the Savoy?
A popular nightclub in Harlem

3. **Singing.** You could play "Name That Tune" with the songs listed in the section "Music Possibilities." (See suggested rules in the chapter "American Popular Song.") Or if your group likes to sing, you could sing several songs together. The following songs would be the easiest and most familiar: "Skip to My Lou," "After the Ball," "Meet Me in St. Louis," and "The Band Played On."

4. **Related Activity.** Ask a local dance studio to have one of their recitals or shows at your facility. Studios that work with children are often looking for new places to perform.

5. **Related Activity.** See these movies that feature dancing: "The Story of Irene and Vernon Castle," "The Gay Divorcee," "Flying Down to Rio," "Top Hat," "An American In Paris," "Swing Time," "Shall We Dance," "Follow the Fleet," "Holiday Inn," "Singin' In the Rain." "That's Dancin'."

6. **Related Activity.** Plan a dance with the residents. See Activity #10 in the chapter on "Big Bands."

DISCUSSION

1. What are some of your earliest memories of dancing? Do any of you remember what your parents thought about dancing?

2. Can any of you share your memories of the first dance you ever attended? Did you go with a group or with a date?

3. Were any of you "flappers," "shebas," or "sheiks"? Do you remember what your parents thought about it? Do you remember where you most liked to go dancing?

4. Did any of you come from a family that didn't believe in dancing? What did young people do when they got together?

5. Did any of you have dancing at your wedding reception? What kind of dancing did you do? Did you like to go dancing after you were married?

6. Did any of you belong to communities or groups where you did particular ethnic or folk dances? Can you tell us about it?

7. Did any of you ever study or teach dancing? Tell us about it.

8. Have any of you ever seen any famous dancers in person? What do you remember?

9. Have any of you ever seen any dances you disapproved of or didn't like as you got older?

10. Did any of you enjoy going to the ballet? What are your memories of that? Do you remember seeing any particular ballets or ballet stars?

You might have a staff member that could give a short demonstration of the Charleston. That would be a great ending for the group.

FASHIONS

IN THE MOOD

Music Possibilities

1. Play an old Fred Astaire record, such as the soundtrack to "Top Hat," since he was one of the most stylish of movie stars in the 1930s. (Presta Sounds has "Exercise with Fred Astaire." See Appendix A.)

2. Songs mentioning clothing:

"Put on Your Old Grey Bonnet"	"Top Hat"
"Five Foot Two, Eyes of Blue"	"Buttons and Bows"
"Button Up Your Overcoat"	"Alice Blue Gown"
"Bell Bottom Trousers"	"Silk Stockings"
"School Days"	"Easter Bonnet"
"Baubles, Bangles, and Beads"	"All of God's Children Got Shoes"

Visual Possibilities

1. Display pictures of fashions. Sources: Old Sears and Wards catalogs; *Good Old Days* magazines; pattern books—many fabric stores sell old ones for a nominal fee; Publishers Central Bureau frequently carries fashion books, vintage paper dolls, or poster reproduction books; library books about fashions; old *Look* or *Life* magazines; Dover Publications' *Everyday Fashions of the Twenties*.

2. Display pictures of movie stars of the 1920s and 1930s in evening clothes. (A good book is Dover Publications' *Hollywood Glamour Portraits*.)

3. If you have a collection of old, fashionable hats, give one to each resident attending to wear during the session.

4. Display some full-page color ads of today's fashions.

5. Suggested objects to display: pattern books, hats, gloves, hat box, hat pins, veils, pocket watch, thermal underwear, boots, or any other fashion accessories you have, particularly if you have some fashions of the past.

You could start or end the session by singing "Alice Blue Gown." Written in 1919, Alice Blue was a light blue color favored by Alice Roosevelt, daughter of Theodore Roosevelt.

ACTIVITIES

1. **Questions**. Using pictures and clothing you have displayed, ask questions about the fashions. Suggestions: Did this article of clothing have a special name? Did you ever wear it? Do you remember when it was popular? Do you remember how much it cost?

2. **Current Fashions**. Share pictures from a recent pattern book (*Vogue* will be the most trendy) or Sears catalog. Tell the participants what is popular now, including some of the more unusual fashions. Ask the participants what they think of today's clothes.

3. **What is it?** Ask the participants to describe these fashions:

> fob - a man's watch chain
> bustle - a pad or frame worn to swell out the fullness at the back of a woman's skirt
> corset - a stiffened undergarment worn by women to give shape to the waist and hips
> union suit - long underwear in one piece
> tam o'shanter - woolen cap with a wide, flat, circular crown and a pompom in the middle
> leggings - a covering for the legs, worn under a skirt
> Eton jacket - A waist-length jacket having broad lapels
> reefer - a close-fitting thick jacket
> bloomers - a woman's garment, with short loose trousers gathered at the knees
> slicker - a long, loose raincoat
> mackintosh - a 2/3 length raincoat
> parasol - a lightweight umbrella used as a shield from sun
> galoshes - buckled rubber boots (they were worn open in the 1920s)
> cloche hat - a woman's hat, bell-shaped and close-fitting
> knickers - loose-fitting short pants gathered at the knee
> hobble skirt - a long skirt that was so straight that the wearer could only take small steps
> peekaboo hat - a 1920s woman's hat that was worn low over the eyes
> empire dress - a dress with a high waistline
> pegtop outfit - a tunic worn over a hobble skirt
> pillbox hat - a woman's low, round hat that sits on the back of the head
> minaret - a belted tunic worn over a narrow skirt
> chemise - a woman's one-piece undergarment, worn under the blouse
> bolero - a short, loose jacket open at the front
> kimono - a loose robe with wide sleeves and a broad sash
> pumps - a shoe with a low heel and no straps

oxfords - a low shoe tied over the instep
shirtwaist - originally, a fancy blouse with long sleeves; now, a dress with collar, long sleeves, and front buttons
pompadour - a long hair style in which the hair is dressed high over the forehead
beret - a round, soft cap with no brim
zoot suit - a man's suit that has baggy, tapered pants and a long, draped coat
bobby socks - short, white socks worn by girls
Mary Janes - plain, low-heeled or flat shoes with a single strap that buckles underneath the ankle
bermuda shorts - straight-legged shorts that stop just above the knee
pedal pushers - straight-legged shorts that stop just below the knee
raglan sleeves - sleeves that are sewn in with seams slanting from neck to underarm
buttonhook - a hook for pulling buttons through buttonholes
turned down hose - in the 1920s, stockings that were folded down just below the knee
knicker dress - short children's dress with bloomers showing from underneath
transformation - artificial hairpiece
raccoon coat - a long, heavy coat made from raccoon fur
Chesterfield - a single-breasted topcoat, usually having a velvet collar
middy - a loose, hip-length woman's blouse with a sailor collar
automobile duster - light overcoat worn while driving
doraine or vanity box - a carrying case used to hold a woman's make-up while out of the house

4. **Related Activity**. Fashion Show: If you are able to find the clothes, you could have a vintage fashion show. Places to check for clothes: (1) participants, families, and staff; (2) thrift stores; (3) a local costume store that might loan some 1920s or Gay 90s clothes in exchange for some free publicity, particularly if you can get newspaper coverage; (4) stores that sell vintage clothing. If you can't find clothing, you might be able to find old hats more easily and have a hat show. The clothes could be displayed by the participants, the staff, or both. Have an M.C. describe each outfit and then serve tea and cookies for refreshments.

5. **Related Activity**. Contact the managers of some local clothing stores to see if one would be willing to give a fashion show at the nursing home.

6. **Related Activity**. Show "Funny Face," a movie about the fashion industry, starring Fred Astaire and Audrey Hepburn.

DISCUSSION

1. Where did you usually shop for clothes...catalogs, department stores, clothing stores? Did you make them yourself? Did you wear the "classics" or did you like to wear whatever was the latest fashion?

2. Did any of you ever rebel against wearing what everyone else was wearing?

3. How did you dress in the 1920s? Did your parents ever disapprove of how you dressed? If so, did any of you ever change clothes after leaving the house?

4. Have any of you ever been to a fashion show? Tell us about it.

IN THE MOOD

Music Possibilities

1. Comic-related music: Theme from "The Green Hornet" ("Flight of the Bumblebee"), theme from "Batman," "Barney Google" (song by Billy Rose), "Popeye the Sailor" song, "Mickey Mouse" song, theme from "The Lone Ranger" ("The William Tell Overture"). (Check children's records and recordings of old radio shows to find these.)

2. Recording of an old radio show about one of these comic strip characters: Buck Rogers in the 25th Century, Flash Gordon, The Green Hornet, The Lone Ranger, Superman, Tarzan, Dick Tracy, Little Orphan Annie, Popeye.

Visual Possibilities

1. Posters of large pictures of cartoon characters such as Mickey Mouse, Donald Duck, Snoopy and the Peanuts gang, Little Orphan Annie, Popeye, Superman.

2. Comic books. (Some used book stores specialize in these.)

3. The Sunday comics section of the newspaper

4. Comic strip collections - Peanuts, B.C., Doonesbury

5. Any merchandising or promotional products from comic strip characters, e.g., Mickey Mouse hat or watch, Snoopy pillow, Little Orphan Annie doll. (Antique shops might have some old ones you could borrow.)

The date listed after each comic strip's name is the year it first appeared. A second date indicates the year it stopped.

ACTIVITIES

1. **To Begin**. You could begin the session by asking the participants to name all the comic strips they can remember. This will start the participants thinking about the topic, as well as give you a good idea of how much they remember about the comics and how much they followed them.

2. **Radio Shows**. If you have tapes of several radio shows featuring comic strip characters (as listed under Music Possibilities #2), play excerpts and let the participants guess what the show or character is.

3. **Comic Strips**. Give each participant a copy of some comic strips, particularly old ones. (*Good Old Days* magazine reprints them and your library probably has books on old comics. *This Fabulous Century* (1930-1940) has a section on the comics.) You can ask, "Do you remember how old you were when this strip was popular? Did you like to read this one?" (The print may be too small for many of them to read.)

4. **Early Comic Strips Today**. A number of early strips are still going today. Clip some of these strips from the Sunday paper and share them with the participants. If you can find a library book that has samples of how they looked when first drawn, it will make an interesting comparison. (You could mount the two strips on cardboard to pass around.) Examples:

"Gasoline Alley," 1918 - originally, a group of men tinkering with their cars
"Snuffy Smith," 1934 - originally a character in the Barney Google strip
"Blondie," 1930 - Blondie was a flapper and Dagwood was her wealthy boyfriend. He was disinherited when he married her and so they settled into typical middle-class family life.
"Ripley's Believe It or Not," 1918
"Mary Worth," 1932 - the first comic strip soap opera, she started as "Apple Mary," the neighborhood busybody
"Henry," 1932 - one of the first pantomime strips, it was imported from Germany
"Donald Duck," 1936 - began as a full-length cartoon in 1928
"Prince Valiant," 1937
"Phantom," 1936
"Archie," 1941

5. **New and Old Comic Strips**. Share some of the comic strips that are most popular today. Then ask the participants if they remember a similar strip from the past.

"Doonesbury". . ."Li'l Abner, 1934, was the first strip of political satire
"Cathy," about a single working woman. . ."Winnie Winkle," 1920, was the first such strip
"Peanuts," 1950. . .The very first comic was called "Hogan's Alley," 1895, and was about a gang of kids, notably The Yellow Kid.
"B.C.," 1958. . ."Alley Oop," 1933, was the first strip about prehistoric times.
"Garfield". . .The first strip about a cat was Krazy Kat, 1911-44, who was always having problems with a brick-throwing mouse named Ignatz.
"Kudzu". . .a born loser like "Barney Google," 1916

40 *Down Memory Lane*

"Tank McNamara," a humorous sports strip. . ."Joe Palooka," 1930, was the first successful strip with an athlete as its central character.

"Spiderman". . ."Tarzan" and "Buck Rogers," both begun in 1929, were the first hero/adventure strips. "Superman," 1938, was the first superhero.

6. **Adaptations**. Tell the participants the plots of the play "Li'l Abner," the movies "Popeye" or "Superman," or the musicals "Annie" or "You're a Good Man, Charlie Brown," playing excerpts from the musicals. If you can find the scripts in the library or used book store, some of the participants might enjoy reading a scene from one of the plays. (Write it in large, bold print for ease of reading.)

7. **Funnies Trivia**. Some extra information is included if you want to expand on it. For more questions, use *Memories, Dreams and Thoughts*. (See Appendix A.)

Who were the two mischievous German immigrant boys who were always getting someone into trouble? **Katzenjammer Kids or Hans and Fritz**, 1912. A copyright dispute gave the kids different names in two newspapers.

What comic strip character, with a sailor suit and a pet bulldog, was later the trademark for a shoe company? **Buster Brown**, 1902-1926. His dog's name was Tige.

What comic strip was about two characters who were of vastly different heights? **"Mutt and Jeff,"** 1907. In 1924, Captain Easy and Wash Tubbs were also of different heights.

Who was the first Jewish character in a comic strip? **Abie Kabibble of "Abie the Agent,"** which ran 1910-32.

What strip was about the "nouveau riche" couple, Maggie and Jiggs? **"Bringing up Father,"** 1913. Maggie was always angry at Jiggs because he wanted to spend time with his poorer friends.

What is a Rube Goldberg? **A complicated contraption that did something simple.** Rube Goldberg drew these "Inventions" of Professor Lucifer Gargonzola Butts periodically for 50 years.

In what strip did Uncle Walt find a baby on his doorstep and name him Skeezix? **"Gasoline Alley,"** 1918 to the present. This is the only strip in which the characters have grown up at the same pace as the readers.

Who was the first comic character to have a popular song written for him? **Barney Google** (and his goo-goo-googly eyes), 1916. He was known for the sayings "heebie-jeebies," "oskywowwow," and "taitched in the haid."

What was the first and most famous police strip? **"Dick Tracy,"** 1931. His girl friend was Tess Trueheart. The strip's premise was that "crime doesn't pay" and it was the first strip in which a character was killed.

Who was Li'l Abner's sweetheart? **Daisy Mae**; it took her 18 years to get him to marry her. Marryin' Sam did the $1.35 ceremony in Dogpatch. The strip began in 1934.

What strip was about the days of King Arthur? **"Prince Valiant,"** 1937 to the present. It was written as a narrative with pictures.

What character said, "I yam what I yam and that's all that I yam." **Popeye**, 1929; his girlfriend was Olive Oyl.

Whose baby, born in 1934, was first named Baby Dumpling and later renamed Alexander? **Blondie**, 1930 to present. Her second child was named Cookie.

At what sport did Joe Palooka, 1930, excel? **Boxing**. His fight manager was named Knobby Walsh.

What is Rex Morgan's profession? **Doctor**. His nurse is named June Gale.

What strip is about a mischievous little boy who always bothers his neighbor Mr. Wilson? **"Dennis the Menace,"** 1951 to the present.

What does Beetle Bailey, 1950, do for a living? **He's a private in the army**. Originally, he was a student.

DISCUSSION

1. Can anyone recall your earliest memory of reading the "funnies"? Did you read them yourself or did someone read them to you?

2. Do any of you remember a favorite comic strip that you could hardly wait to read each day? Were there comic strips that any of you *hated*?

3. Did any of you have a favorite comic strip that you later listened to on the radio or saw in the movies or even on television?

4. Did you ever buy comic books for your children or grandchildren? (They were first published in 1934.) Do you remember what any of the favorites were?

5. If any of you lived in New York City, do you remember hearing Mayor LaGuardia read the Sunday comics during the newspaper strike?

6. Did any of you, or your children, ever send away for products offered free in the comics or by comic characters on the radio? Have you ever bought any such merchandising products in the stores? Do you remember what they were?

7. Did any of you read the "funnies" first before any other part of the paper? Do any of you still read the "funnies"? What are your favorites?

      When I led this session, the participants especially enjoyed hearing several humorous comic strips read to them. This is a good way to end the session or the strips could be used throughout the session. To save time in the session, pick these particular strips out in advance.

The GOLDEN AGE of TELEVISION

IN THE MOOD

Music Possibilities

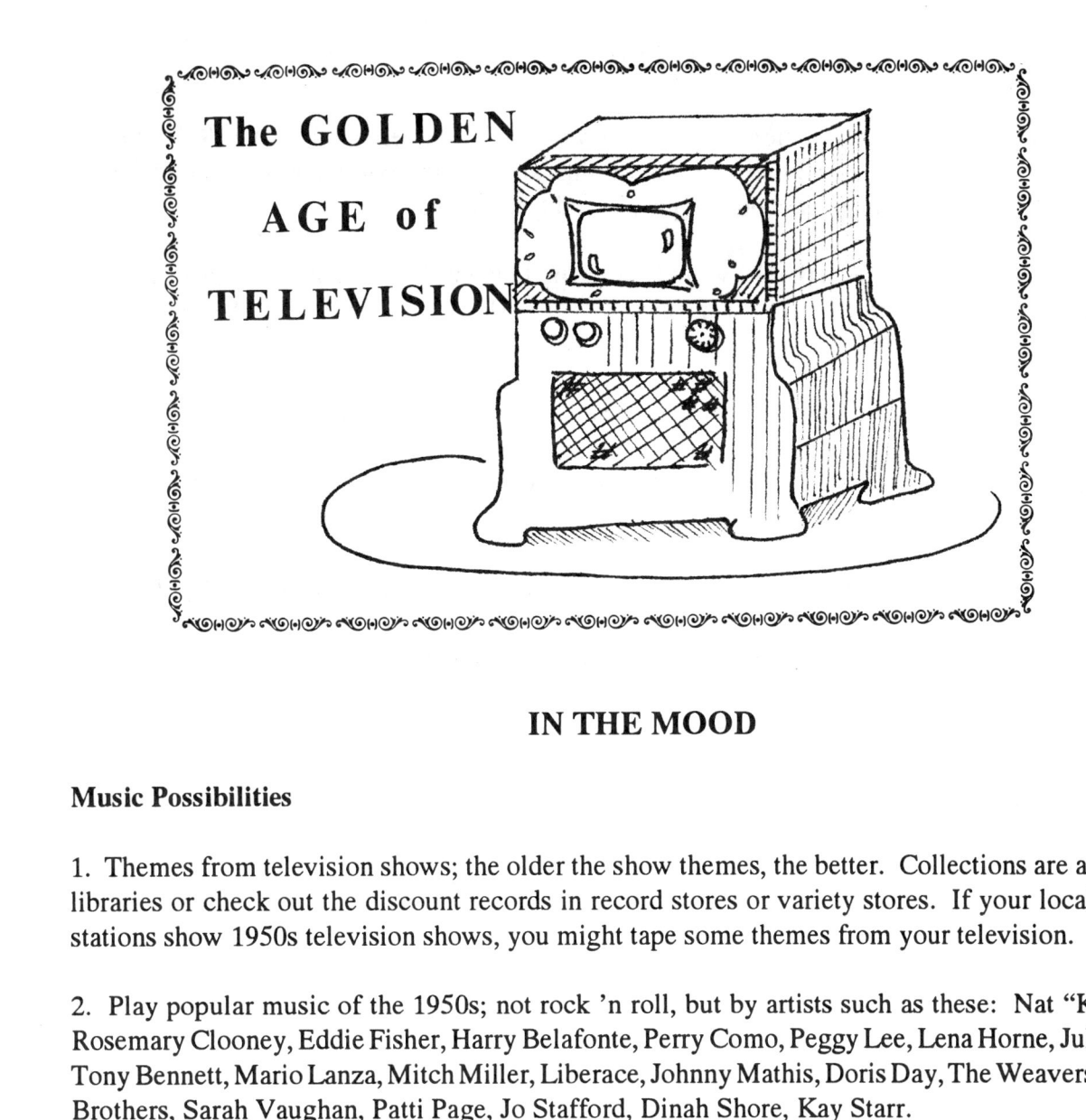

1. Themes from television shows; the older the show themes, the better. Collections are available in libraries or check out the discount records in record stores or variety stores. If your local television stations show 1950s television shows, you might tape some themes from your television.

2. Play popular music of the 1950s; not rock 'n roll, but by artists such as these: Nat "King" Cole, Rosemary Clooney, Eddie Fisher, Harry Belafonte, Perry Como, Peggy Lee, Lena Horne, Julie London, Tony Bennett, Mario Lanza, Mitch Miller, Liberace, Johnny Mathis, Doris Day, The Weavers, The Mills Brothers, Sarah Vaughan, Patti Page, Jo Stafford, Dinah Shore, Kay Starr.

Visual Possibilities

1. Pictures of early television personalities, such as these: Lucille Ball, Desi Arnaz, Sid Caesar, Imogene Coca, Jackie Gleason, Milton Berle, Dave Garroway, Jack Lescoulie, Huntley and Brinkley, Jack LaLanne, Edward R. Murrow, Ed Sullivan, Phil Silvers, Ozzie and Harriet Nelson, Audrey Meadows, Wally Cox, Steve Allen, Garry Moore, Art Linkletter, Ernie Kovacs, George Gobel, Arthur Godfrey, Ted Mack, Lawrence Welk, Red Skelton, Tennessee Ernie Ford, Walter Cronkite, Perry Como, Dinah Shore, Phil Silvers, Arthur and Kathryn Murray, John Cameron Swayze.

2. Large picture of an old television set; it had a large cabinet and a very small screen. Check out ads in old *Life* or *Look* magazines or a library book on television's "Golden Age."

3. Picture of a television camera.

4. One of today's mini-televisions.

ACTIVITIES

1. **To Begin**. Ask the participants to name all the television shows they remember from the 1950s. What were their favorites? Show any pictures you have found and ask the participants to identify the personalities and what they remember about the people and their shows.

2. **Theme Songs**. Play themes from the shows and ask the participants if they remember the show and who starred in it. Easily identifiable ones: "I Love Lucy," "The Honeymooners," "Jack Benny Show" ("Love in Bloom"), "Today Show" ("Misty").

3. **Local Television**. Invite someone from your local television station to come and talk to the participants about television, especially someone who has been involved in it for 20 years or more. Ask the guest to talk about (1) how television has changed over the years and (2) what goes on behind the scenes to make up a television show.

4. **Play-reading**. If your group likes drama and play-reading, have them read part of the script for one of the early shows. Look in the library or used book store for one and copy the parts in large print. *This Fabulous Century* (1950-1960) has three short excerpts. Here are some of the classics:

    "No Time for Sergeants"   "Marty"
    "Bang the Drum Slowly"   "Visit to a Small Planet"
    "A Doll's House"   "The Bachelor Party"

5. **Television Trivia**

    Who was known as Mr. Television?
    Milton Berle
    Who was the star of "Your Show of Shows"?
    Sid Caesar
    What flamboyant pianist started out on an early, sedate television show?
    Liberace
    The Boob Tube, The Idiot Box, and The Light That Failed were all nicknames given to what?
    Television
    On what quiz show did four panelists try to guess someone's unusual occupation?
    "What's My Line?"
    What was the first puppet show on television, hosted by Fran Allison?
    "Kukla, Fran, and Ollie"
    What American opera was commissioned for television, appearing first in 1951?
    "Amahl and the Night Visitors"
    In what musical play, broadcast on television, did Mary Martin fly across the stage?
    "Peter Pan"
    What major television commentator, in his news show, "See It Now", was the first to launch an attack on Senator Joseph McCarthy in 1954?
    Edward R. Murrow
    What was the first crime show on television, with a cop named Joe Friday?
    "Dragnet"

What television comedian/personality, who was the first host of the "Tonight Show," used the "Man on the Street" interview?
> **Steve Allen**

What TV personality, also an early host of the "Tonight Show", was known for saying, "I kid you not."
> **Jack Parr**

What was the name of the show that starred Jackie Gleason and Audrey Meadows as a bus driver and his wife?
> **"The Honeymooners"**

What weekly news show featured a panel of journalists questioning a prominent politician?
> **"Meet the Press"**

Who was the television personality that played the ukelele and fired Julius La Rosa on a live show?
> **Arthur Godfrey**

What television star was known for ending her show by throwing a big kiss to the audience?
> **Dinah Shore**

What Senate investigation fizzled due to the glare of live coverage by television?
> **The Army/McCarthy Hearings**

Who was the host of "You Bet Your Life"?
> **Groucho Marx** (his announcer was George Fenniman)

Who was J. Fred Muggs?
> **Dave Garroway's chimpanzee companion on "The Today Show"**

What television show was about a school teacher played by Eve Arden?
> **"Our Miss Brooks"**

For what was Charles Van Doren famous?
> **He won thousands in the quiz show "21"; later it was discovered that the show was rigged.**

Who gave the famous "Checkers Speech" on television?
> **Then Vice President Richard Nixon**

What was Art Linkletter's afternoon show called?
> **"House Party," later "People are Funny"**

What was the name of Ed Sullivan's show when it first appeared on television in 1948?
> **"Toast of the Town"**

Who was known for saying, "Well, I'll be a dirty bird"?
> **George Gobel**

What was the name of the show in which a hidden camera showed the reactions of ordinary people to extraordinary things?
> **"Candid Camera"**

On what show did Ralph Edwards feature a surprise life story of a member of the audience?
> **"This Is Your Life"**

Who took over Major Bowes' "Original Amateur Hour"?
> **Ted Mack**

What personality ended his show each time by holding up his palm and saying "Peace"?
> **Dave Garroway, on "The Today Show"**

6. **Television Today.** Tell the participants about television technology of today, such as the pocket television, wide screen televisions with VCRs, satellite dishes, etc., and bring in pictures, examples, and current prices, if you can.

7. **Related Activity**. If you have a VCR, rent a copy of two to three old television shows and show them to the participants. If you don't have a VCR, some dramas were later made into feature films and are available through library film services. Look for these films: "Marty," "The Miracle Worker," and "No Time for Sergeants."

DISCUSSION

1. Can any of you remember the first time you saw television? Where were you? Do you remember what you saw? What did you think about it? Did you think it would become so popular that it would replace radio as the main home entertainment?

2. Do any of you remember when you first bought a television? What did it look like? Do you remember what it cost? How much did you watch it? Did you continue to listen to the radio?

3. What historical events do any of you remember seeing on television in the early years? Did you like seeing the news on television or did you prefer the radio or reading about it in the newspaper? (Noteworthy events to ask about: 1952 political conventions that nominated Dwight Eisenhower and Adlai Stevenson, McCarthy-Army hearings, Inauguration of John Kennedy, Elvis Presley on Ed Sullivan's show.)

4. Have any of you ever been in a television audience? What did you see? Have any of you ever been on television or helped put on a television show? Tell us about it.

5. What are your favorite television shows of today?

HOME SWEET HOME

IN THE MOOD

Music Possibilities

1. Music of 1890 to 1925, particularly recordings of a piano and a vocalist together.

2. Have a music box playing or a recording of one. (If you have a music box, one of the residents can keep it going as the others enter.)

3. Ragtime piano music (Scott Joplin). You might be able to find someone who can play it live.

4. Mitch Miller sing-along records, especially if the songs are from the early part of the century.

5. Songs about home:

"I'll Take you Home Again, Kathleen"	"Home Sweet Home"
"Any Place I Hang My Hat Is Home"	"Old Folks at Home"
"Keep the Home Fires Burning"	"My Old Kentucky Home"
"Show Me the Way to Go Home"	"Home for the Holidays"
"My Indiana Home"	

Visual Possibilities

1. Use objects, or pictures of objects, found in the home in the early part of this century. Some of the participants or their families might have original ones to share. You can draw pictures or look for pictures in these resources: *Good Old Days* magazines, *This Fabulous Century*, reprints of old Sears or Wards catalogs, *The Encyclopedia of Collectibles* by Time-Life books. (See Appendix A.)

Suggestions:

cross-stitch	sampler	spittoon
family Bible	stereoscope	Brownie camera
shaving mug and razor	pump organ	player piano
old sheet music	milk bottles	wood-burning stove
"Home Sweet Home" sign	iron skillet	quilt
wooden spoons	canning jars	pocket watch
old radio	old telephone	rainbarrel
manual typewriter	grandfather clock	coffee grinder
gramophone	chamber pot	

2. Put these sayings on large posters on the wall:

"There's no place like home"
"Home is where the heart is"
"Any place I hang my hat is home"
"Home sweet home"
"People in glass houses shouldn't throw stones"

ACTIVITIES

1. **Theme Song**. You can start or end the session by singing "Home Sweet Home" or by listening to a recording of it.

2. **Objects from the Home**. Talk about the objects or pictures of objects that you have. Ask questions like these: What is it? For what was it used? Who used it most of the time?

3. **Household Items**. If you have *Good Old Days* magazines or old catalogs, copy ads for household items and give one to each participant, particularly for objects that are no longer common. Ask each participant to talk about the object(s) in their ad, taking note of the prices. If you can't find ads, you could name the objects and have the participants explain what they are. Examples of items no longer in use:

treadle sewing machine	flypaper	wire rug beater
shaving mug	tobacco or cigar jar	mustache cup
fountain pens	curling or waving iron	baby tender
ottoman	parlor heater	flour sieve
coal hod	ice box	coffee mill
cherry seeder	wringer washer	davenport
bridge lamp	porch swing	gateleg table
steam radiator	beaded lamp shade	ink stand

For comparison, you could show ads from a current catalog or magazine, especially for objects that are an updated version of something common 60 years ago; for instance, telephones having several special features on them, microwave ovens, sewing machines, refrigerators, electric juicers, food processors.

4. **Rooms.** Ask the participants to name all the rooms in the houses in which they lived while young. Next, ask them to name all the objects that might be found in the rooms, one room at a time (kitchen, dining room, bedroom, nursery, root cellar, parlor, etc.). You might write them down on a blackboard or easel pad as they are named. As an alternative, you could ask the participants to name objects from the house by letters of the alphabet (all objects beginning with a, then b, then c, etc.). You might want to make a list for yourself ahead of time or consult *Keep Minds Alert*. (See Appendix A.)

5. **Home Events.** Ask the participants their memories of major events that took place regularly in the home, such as these:

> wash day - wringer washers, washboards, clotheslines
> ironing - starch collars, heating the iron on the stove
> long winter evenings - reading, needlework, family in one room to keep warm, looking at stereoscopes or kaleidoscopes, listening to the radio or to the Victrola
> summers on the front porch - rocking chairs, talking to neighbors, making ice cream, keeping cool, lemonade
> family music times - player pianos, sheet music, pump organs
> spring cleaning - feather dusters, rug beating, turning the mattresses
> quilting bees - patchwork, batting, quilting frames
> cooking and baking - favorite recipes, wood stoves
> religious days - going to church or synagogue, wearing one's best clothes
> when company came - best china, napkin rings, best behavior
> gardening - favorite flowers and vegetables to plant, weeding, taking the best to the county fair
> canning - mason jars, steamer, seals, jams and preserves
> deliveries - mail, ice, milk, packages

6. **Collections of Objects.** If there is a museum in your town or city that has objects from early twentieth-century homes, contact their education or outreach office. They might have some smaller objects that could be borrowed or brought by one of their staff to be shared. Some antique shops might loan some small, unbreakable items that would be appropriate. (They might ask for a deposit for their safe return.) The antique dealers might also know of some local collectors that could be contacted and asked to share some of their collection. Items can also be found at estate sales, particularly if the owners had lived in the same house for many years.

7. **Songs.** Sing some old songs that might have been sung in the home as a family, such as (1) old Gospel hymns, (2) ethnic music, (3) popular songs, such as by Stephen Foster, or these:

"Down by the Old Mill Stream"	"Love's Old Sweet Song"
"Juanita"	"The Land Where We'll Never Grow Old"
"Sweet and Low"	"Brighten the Corner Where You Are"
"Little Gypsy Sweetheart"	"Whispering Hope"

Before the session is held, you might poll the participants to find out what songs they remember the best. Be prepared to make suggestions when you ask them.

8. **Related Activity.** See a movie about home life at the turn of the century, such as "Life With Father" or "Cheaper by the Dozen."

Down Memory Lane 49

9. **Related Activity**. If you have a cooking class, get a recipe for a baked item (like an apple pie) from the participants and make it in conjunction with this session. You could either get the recipe during the course of the session and make it later in the week, or make the dish before the session and then serve it at the end of this session.

DISCUSSION

1. Can any of you tell us your earliest memory of your home and your family? Did your parents ever tell you about what it was like when you were born?

2. Did you live with only your parents and siblings or were there other relatives in the home, too?

3. Who can tell us something about your mother? Your father? Your brothers or sisters? Who do you most resemble? Who was your biggest influence?

4. Does anyone remember having pictures taken of your family? Did your family have its own camera?

5. Did anyone have a telephone when growing up? Was it always a party line? Did the operator ever listen to your calls?

6. Does anyone remember if there was running water in your first home? How many of you had outdoor toilets? Was every bedroom equipped with a chamber pot? Does anyone know what a W.C. is? (Water closet, a polite word for an indoor bathroom.) Do any of you remember when you first had indoor plumbing? (Some groups might be a bit embarrassed by these particular questions.)

7. What songs do you remember your mother or grandmother teaching you? (Sing one!)

IN THE MOOD

Music Possibilities

1. Recording of nickelodeon or carousel music or of piano rolls.

2. Music of the 1920s, the greatest decade for ice cream. (See Appendix B for song suggestions.)

3. Recording of a band concert, like in an old-fashioned concert in the park.

4. A pianist playing old popular favorites from 1900-1930.

5. If you can find a copy of "I Scream You Scream We All Scream for Ice Cream," play or sing it with the participants as part of your introduction. If you can't find it, you could write the phrase on a poster for display in your activity room.

Visual Possibilities - Make your activity room look like an old-fashioned ice cream parlor.

1. Checkered table cloth on an activity table.

2. Large drawings or photos of ice cream cones or ice cream sodas.

3. A large price list on the wall for various ice cream treats. Example of the menu from a soda fountain of the 1920s:

Deluxe Club Sandwich, 50 cents	Pie, 10 cents
Peach Ice Cream, 15 cents	Pie a la mode, 15 cents
Ice Cream Soda, 25 cents	Cake, 10 cents

4. Put the words "Ice Cream Parlour" on the activity room door.

5. Put up a picture or drawing of an old soda fountain.

6. Display a hand-cranked ice cream maker.

ACTIVITIES

1. **Ice Cream Treats**. Make large-print copies of a typical menu from a 1920s ice cream parlor and give them out. (See Visual Possibilities #3.) Ask the participants what their choice would be. You could also ask them if they know how different kinds of ice cream treats should be made. Examples:

> **Chocolate ice-cream soda** ("black and white") - whipping cream, chocolate syrup, soda water, and vanilla ice cream

> **Ice cream sundae** - vanilla ice cream, fruit or chocolate syrup, and whipped cream

> **Root beer-chocolate float** ("brown cow") - whipping cream, chocolate syrup, root beer, and vanilla ice cream

> **Chocolate malted with chocolate ice cream** ("burn one all the way") - whipping cream, chocolate syrup, malted milk powder, and chocolate ice cream, with nutmeg on top

> **Chocolate egg cream** ("Square meal") - an egg, whipping cream, chocolate syrup, and chocolate ice cream

> **Strawberry milk shake** - fresh strawberries, whipping cream, vanilla or strawberry ice cream

2. **The Soda Jerk**. The soda jerk, working at a soda fountain, was a revered person. Boys would take any job in a drug store in order to work their way up to that position. Give some examples of typical soda jerk language from the list below and see if the participants can guess what the terms mean. Some groups of participants might enjoy inventing their own soda jerk language. Examples:

> cow juice - milk
> H20 - water
> OJ - orange juice
> yum-yum - sugar
> looseness - prunes
> nervous pudding - gelatin
> hold the hail - no ice
> cold spot - iced tea
>
> fizz - carbonated water
> lumber - toothpick
> suds - root beer
> white cow - vanilla milk shake
> M.D. - Dr. Pepper
> on wheels - to go
> hot spot - tea

3. **Pictures**. If you can find a good book about the history of ice cream, show pictures of old ice cream parlors, soda fountains, Good Humor trucks, etc., and encourage the participants to share their memories of what is in the pictures. A good resource on the subject is *The Great American Ice Cream Book* by Paul Dickson (Atheneum, 1973).

4. **Make ice cream by hand**. The ice cream freezes best if you can mix the ingredients one day, refrigerate it, and then make it into ice cream the next. Most ice cream makers come with a list of instructions and recipes. Here is a basic recipe for vanilla ice cream that works well and needs no cooking:

Combine the following ingredients in a bowl and mix thoroughly with a mixer:
    4 eggs   1/2 pint whipping cream   1 cup sugar
    2 tbsp vanilla   1/4 teaspoon salt

Pour into the ice cream container. Add two cans of Eagle Brand sweetened, condensed milk and stir well. Add whole milk to the "fill" line on the ice cream container and stir. Makes four quarts. If you add pureed fruit, you can cut down on the sugar.

5. **Make ice cream malteds**. You can buy vanilla ice cream for this activity, or you can have a group of residents hand crank ice cream one day, freeze it solid overnight, and then make it into malteds the next day. Here are the material needed and instructions for the malteds:

    hand mixer or egg beater   ice cream
    malted milk crystals   chocolate syrup
    milk   cherries
    whipped cream (in an aerosol can)   nutmeg
    napkins   straws
    large mixing spoon   large mixing bowl
    plastic parfait glasses
      (sold in paper or party stores)

The amount needed of each ingredient varies with the size of your group. Estimate how many people you expect and have enough ice cream for about 1/2 cup for each.

If you're working with a small group, you can meet around a table and all help to make the malteds. With a large group, a few participants can help to make the malteds for everyone. You might find it easier to make one big malted in a large bowl and pour it into individual glasses.

Directions: Put the ice cream, softened somewhat, in a large bowl. Pour in some malted milk crystals, chocolate syrup, and a little milk. Blend with the mixer or egg beater. Add more syrup and malt as needed for the taste you like. Add more milk to make it as thick or as thin as desired. When blended, pour into individual glasses. Put whipped cream and a cherry on top and sprinkle with nutmeg. Add a straw and enjoy! Upbeat 1920s music played during this entire activity adds to the fun.

DISCUSSION

1. Do any of you remember the days before refrigerators, when everyone had ice boxes? Where did you get your ice? What do you remember about the ice man's visits?

2. Did every town have an ice cream parlor or a soda fountain? Do any of you remember how much it cost for an ice cream cone? What was your favorite ice cream treat?

3. Did you usually make ice cream or buy it? Do any of you remember how you made it? If you lived in the city, where could you buy ice cream? Can any of you remember the name of your town's ice cream parlor or soda fountain? Was that a good place to have a date with someone? (Tell the participants the names of the ice cream parlors in your town today.)

4. Do any of you remember having Eskimo pies? Did any of you ever buy ice cream from the Good Humor truck?

5. Did any of you ever live in a town that harvested ice in the winter and stored it in the ground for use in the summer? Did your town have an ice cream festival in the summer? Tell us about it.

6. If you were in charge of coming up with new flavors for a large ice cream company, what would be some interesting flavors? (Call a local ice cream store, such as Baskin-Robbins, and ask for the names of some of their more exotic flavors to share with the group.)

If you don't make ice cream, serve Good Humor bars or Eskimo pies.

Here's a joke for ending the session: "What do you call a person who runs an ice cream truck? A Sundae driver"

IN THE MOOD

Music Possibilities

1. There are dozens of record collections of themes from the movies by orchestras. However, the participants will enjoy it more if you can find a collection from movies made between 1930 and 1950. Here are some early Academy Award winners:

1934, "The Continental"	1943, "You'll Never Know"
1935, "Lullaby Of Broadway"	1944, "Swinging On a Star"
1936, "The Way You Look Tonight"	1945, "It Might As Well Be Spring"
1937, "Sweet Leilani"	1946, "On the Atchison, Topeka and the Santa Fe"
1938, "Thanks For the Memory"	1947, "Zip-a-dee-doo-dah"
1939, "Over the Rainbow"	1948, "Buttons and Bows"
1940, "When You Wish Upon a Star"	1949, "Baby, It's Cold Outside"
1941, "The Last Time I Saw Paris"	1950, "Mona Lisa"
1942, "White Christmas"	

2. Play a collection of songs from the movies sung by a popular vocalist, such as Bing Crosby, Frank Sinatra, Judy Garland, or Fred Astaire.

3. Play the soundtrack of a well-known musical that was made into a movie, e.g., "Oklahoma," "Carousel," "Showboat."

4. Presta Sounds has several movie soundtracks, including "Easter Parade," and there is a tape called "Name That Movie." (See Appendix A.)

Visual Possibilities

1. Display movie posters. Book stores and novelty shops often carry these, especially "Gone With the Wind" and "Casablanca."

2. Display large pictures of movie stars from 1920-1950 or give smaller ones to each resident who attends. You can find pictures in these publications: *Good Old Days* magazines, *This Fabulous Century*, old *Life* magazines, and some of the books sold by Publishers Central Bureau. (See Appendix A.) You can probably find some library books or some used books with good pictures, too. Dover Publications has a good photo book called *Hollywood Glamor Portraits*.

ACTIVITIES

1. **Movie Songs**. If you can get some original recordings of stars singing songs from movies, play several excerpts and let the participants guess who is singing. Examples:

> **Judy Garland**: "Over the Rainbow," "The Boy Next Door," "The Trolley Song"
> **Bing Crosby**: "Swinging On a Star," "White Christmas," "The Bells Of St. Mary's," "Too-ra-loo-ra-loo-ra"
> **Shirley Temple**: "On the Good Ship Lollipop"
> **Fred Astaire**: "Top Hat," "Funny Face," "Cheek to Cheek"
> **Maurice Chevalier**: "Mimi," "Gigi"

2. **Pictures**. If you can find pictures of movie stars of 1920-1950, ask the participants to identify them. If you give a picture to each resident who attends, see if that participant can identify the star. Ask questions of the group about each one, such as these: Was this star in silent movies or talkies? For what was she/he best known? Do you remember any movies in which this person starred?

3. **Silent Films**

    A. Ask the participants to name the silent film stars they remember. If you can find pictures, show them and let the participants guess who they are. Examples: Harold Lloyd, Charlie Chaplin, Mary Pickford, Douglas Fairbanks, Errol Flynn, Rudolph Valentino, Lillian Gish, John Gilbert, Fatty Arbuckle. Ask the participants who their favorites were, comic and romantic.

    B. Ask the participants if they remember the names of any silent films. Examples: "The Sheik of Araby," "The Little Tramp," "The Hunchback of Notre Dame," "The Thief of Baghdad."

    C. The first full-length film that had talking and singing was Al Jolson's "The Jazz Singer." Ask the participants if they remember seeing this. Did any of them think, at the time, that it would mean the end of silent films?

    D. Show a short silent film. Many libraries carry some in 8mm or 16mm or in video. Screen the film first so that you can check the quality and can give an introduction to it.

    E. **Related Activity**. Show Mel Brooks' "Silent Movie," a 1970s silent film.

4. Movie Trivia.

In 1926, the biggest box office draw was a German Shepherd dog...what was his name?
> **Rin Tin Tin**

What was the name of the madcap police officers from silent films?
> **The Keystone Kops**

What was a nickelodeon?
> **The first movie "theater."** It cost five cents to see about an hour's worth of one-reelers.

What was the first full-length talkie?
> **"The Jazz Singer"** with Al Jolson (1927)

What two stars danced together and sang in "The Gay Divorcee" and "Top Hat"?
> **Fred Astaire and Ginger Rogers**

The operettas "Rose-Marie" and "Naughty Marietta" featured which singing stars?
> **Nelson Eddy and Jeanette MacDonald**

What star did King Kong love?
> **Fay Wray** (1933)

What singing-dancing star performed with fruit on her hats?
> **Carmen Miranda**

Who starred in the Andy Hardy movies?
> **Mickey Rooney**

Who played Nick and Nora Charles in the "Thin Man" movies?
> **Myrna Loy and William Powell**

What were these: *Silver Screen, Photoplay, Motion Picture,* and *Screen Romances*?
> **Movie fan magazines**

Who was "America's Sweetheart"?
> **Mary Pickford**

Who was "America's Little Sweetheart"?
> **Shirley Temple**

Who was "America's Favorite Cowboy," singing "Back in the Saddle Again"?
> **Gene Autry**

In the 1938 Cary Grant movie "Bringing Up Baby," who was Baby?
> **A leopard**

Who was known as "The Vamp"?
> **Theda Bara**

Who was known as "The 'It' Girl"?
> **Clara Bow**

Who said "I want to be alone"?
> **Greta Garbo**

What movie about the south starred Clark Gable and Vivien Leigh?
> **"Gone With the Wind"**

Who was the Olympic swimmer who made several swimming spectaculars?
> **Esther Williams**

What famous movie was made about the life of William Randolph Hearst?
> **"Citizen Kane"**

What Walt Disney movie, in 1937, was the first full-length cartoon?
> **"Snow White and the Seven Dwarfs"**

Who were the four zany brothers who made movies in the 1930s?
> **Groucho, Zeppo, Harpo, and Chico Marx**

What child star played in "National Velvet"?
> **Elizabeth Taylor**

Who was Spencer Tracy's favorite leading lady?
> **Katherine Hepburn** (They starred together in nine movies.)

Who said "Here's lookin' at you, kid."
> **Humphrey Bogart to Ingrid Bergman in "Casablanca"**

Who played Dorothy in "The Wizard of Oz"?
> **Judy Garland**

Who was the Sheik?
> **Rudolph Valentino**

DISCUSSION

1. Did any of you ever go to a nickelodeon? Do you remember what you saw?

2. Did any of you have a silent screen idol? Do any of you remember when Valentino died?

3. Do any of you remember the music played at silent films? Were familiar melodies or new ones played? Did any of you ever provide the music at silent films?

4. Have any of you ever seen any early film stars in person? Were you thrilled or disappointed? Have any of you ever asked anyone for autographs?

5. Do any of you remember the fan magazines? Did you read them? Did you believe what was in them? Did any of you ever join a star's fan club?

6. Did any of you ever aspire to be an actor or an actress? Were you ever in any plays or movies?

7. How much did movies cost in the 1920s and 1930s? Were movies shown every day or just on weekends? Did the whole family go or did you go with friends? Were movies allowed to be shown on Sundays?

8. Did any of you have a favorite male or female screen idol from a talking movie? Do you remember any of his or her movies?

9. Does anyone remember the most recent movie they saw in a movie theater? Do you think movies have improved over the years?

There are more trivia questions in *Memories, Dreams and Thoughts*, the library is filled with books about the movies, and you can find anecdotes about movies and movie stars in *Good Old Days* magazines.

MOVING ALONG

This is a very broad subject. You could do a series of sessions on the different kinds of transportation, you could concentrate on one or two sections that seem to be the most interesting to your group, or you could do one session that would touch briefly on each section.

IN THE MOOD

Music Possibilities

1. Appropriate songs to sing or to play:

    "In My Merry Oldsmobile"   "Trolley Song"
    "Bicycle Built For Two"   "Lucky Lindy"
    "Cruising Down the River"   "Row, Row, Row"
    "On the Good Ship Lollipop"   "Moonlight Bay"
    "Surrey With the Fringe On Top"   "Toot, Toot, Tootsie"
    "On a Slow Boat To China"   "Chattanooga Choo Choo"
    "Red Sails In the Sunset"   "Flying Down To Rio"
    "I've Been Workin' On the Railroad" "Row Your Boat"
    "Come, Josephine, In My Flying Machine" "Coming In On a Wing and a Prayer"

2. If you have a sound effects record, play recordings of various kinds of transportation.

Visual Possibilities

1. Pictures of pre-1950 cars, streetcars, airplanes, luxury liners, trains, bicycles, unicycles, ferry boats, subways, etc. Posters of vintage cars, trains, and planes are available from Giant Photo. (Appendix A.)

2. Models of pre-1950 cars or airplanes. Matchbox cars or other children's toys.

ACTIVITIES

1. **Cars.** Start the session by singing "In My Merry Oldsmobile." Ask the participants if any of them ever owned an Oldsmobile and what it was like to ride in one.

2. **Cars.** Ask the participants to name all the cars they remember owning. If you have found large pictures of old cars, show them to the participants and see if they remember what kind of car it is. If the participants can't remember very many kinds of cars, name some of the early companies to jog their memories. Examples: Nash, Hudson, La Salle, Overland, Graham, De Soto, Zephyr, Ford, Packard, Pierce-Arrow, Studebaker, Hupmobile, Duesenberg, Kaiser, Scripps-Booth.

3. **Cars.** There are people all over the U.S. who have one or more vintage cars. You could invite someone to drive his or her car to the nursing home to show it off, as well as to talk about the history of this particular car.

4. **Costs of Cars.** Ask the participants if they remember what it cost to buy a car in the early days. Here are some sample costs:

    1903, Cadillac - $750
    1905, Ford Model F - $1,200
    1918, Ford Model T - $400
    1920s, Chevrolet Sports Roadster - $555
    Late 1920s, Pontiac 6 - $745
    1930s, Cadillac V-16 - $5,350 to $15,000
    1940, La Salle - $2,295 to $2,875

5. **Discussion about Cars.** Ask the participants to share what it was like to ride in one of the early cars. Ask them if they remember any of these things:

    goggles
    rumble seats
    horseless carriages (The early cars were just horse buggies with motors in them.)
    punctures and how to change them
    cranking the engine (Usually only men were strong enough to get the car started by cranking.)
    muddy roads
    getting a driver's license
    learning to drive
    isinglas windows
    running boards
    tire chains
    gas stations (Many had glass cylinders so you could watch the gas go into your car.)
    when cars only came in black (pre-1925. Black paint dried the quickest so it was used in order
        to meet the great demand for cars.)
    1920s sports cars
    riding in a "tin lizzie" (Model T)
    Who had the first car in town?

6. **Boats and Ships**. In some areas, participants may not ever have been on water, except perhaps in a rowboat. In other places, sailboats, cruisers, fishing boats, or riding on ocean liners may have been common. Through discussion, explore the participants' experiences on boats or ships. Show any pictures you have to aid in the discussion. Suggested topics:

>   making a living on boats
>   living on a houseboat
>   sailing on a ship to war
>   sailing on an ocean liner
>   sailing on a sailboat
>   riding a gondola in Venice
>   going canoeing - for romance, for travel
>   riding boats through a "Tunnel of Love" at an amusement park
>   riding on a ferry
>   hearing news about the sinking of "The Titanic"
>   fishing from a boat

7. **Trains**. Show pictures of any trains you can find and ask the participants to share their memories of the following:

>   Pullman cars and berths (sleeping cars)
>   Pullman porters (men who waited on the passengers)
>   "baggage smashers" (men who put cargo into the baggage car)
>   dining car
>   walking in a moving train
>   "whistle stop tours" (politicians stopped in each little town and made a speech from the rear platform)
>   "going on the bum" or "riding the rails" (hitchhiking on trains)
>   train whistles
>   dust on the train
>   what it was like to take a long trip on a train

8. **Airplanes**. Show any pictures or models of early airplanes you have found. Ask the participants to share their memories of the following:

>   the first time they saw an airplane
>   their first airplane ride
>   barnstorming (pilots flew across the country in short flights, earning money by taking people up for rides)
>   air shows (pilots did airplane stunts for a crowd)
>   Lindbergh's nonstop, solo flight to France, 1927
>   memories of piloting a plane
>   Amelia Earhart, her flights and mysterious disappearance
>   Richard Byrd's flight over the North and South poles

9. **Airplanes**. If you have an airport in your town, invite a local pilot to come in and talk about what it's like to pilot an airplane today. If you can find someone of retirement age, that person can talk about how everything has changed.

Down Memory Lane 61

10. **Before Cars**. Many of the participants may remember the days before cars were common, especially if they lived in a rural area. Encourage the participants, through discussion, to share their long-ago memories of horses and bicycles.

> unicycles
> bicycle races
> tandem bicycles (Sing "Bicycle Built for Two.")
> riding in a "one-horse open sleigh" in the winter
> side saddles for women
> livery stables
> horse buggies

11. **Streetcars, Subways, Trolleys**. Play "The Trolley Song" (originally from the movie "Meet Me in St. Louis"). Many cities have street car museums. You could take a field trip there or just go yourself to get information. Show pictures of any streetcars, trolleys, or subways you have found and ask the participants to share their memories of the following:

> fares - how much, fare register, fare box
> conductor and motorman - what they did
> riding to school
> advertising placards in the cars
> standee straps
> streetcar gongs (warning), bells (the motorman's signal for stopping and starting), buzzers (for passengers to signal for stops)
> roller destination signs
> hitching rides on the back of a streetcar
> the final day of a streetcar operation in town

12. **Related Activity**. Show movies featuring transportation in the early part of this century. Suggestions: "The Spirit of St. Louis," "Those Magnificent Men in Their Flying Machines," "The Great Waldo Pepper," "The Great Race."

Dover Publications has several books that contain pictures of early modes of transport. Also, see *This Fabulous Century*. (See Appendix A.)

IN THE MOOD

Music Possibilities

1. Play the soundtrack to Meredith Willson's musical "The Music Man," which is about small town life in Iowa at the early part of this century.

2. Play a recording of band music, such as John Philip Sousa marches, patriotic songs, or arrangements of popular songs of 1890-1920. Band concerts in the park were a popular way of spending an afternoon or evening.

3. Play songs about different towns or cities. Examples:

"I Left My Heart In San Francisco"	"Chicago"
"Chattanooga Choo Choo"	"The Sidewalks of New York"
"I've Got a Gal in Kalamazoo"	"Meet me in St. Louis"
"Give My Regards to Broadway"	"Moon Over Miami"

4. A good beginning or ending song is "Dear Hearts and Gentle People."

Visual Possibilities - Pictures of the following: soda fountain, striped barber pole, firehouse, American flag, house with a picket fence, bandstand in the park, church, red schoolhouse, postman, fireworks, town square, Woolworth's 5 and 10 Cent Store.

Places to find pictures: (1) You could draw some of these places or things on poster board and put them on display. (2) You could find pictures in *Good Old Days* magazines or in library books and make copies to give participants as they come. (3) You could display a large flag and make a striped barber pole with poster board and construction paper or paint.

ACTIVITIES

1. **Buildings**. Take photographs of buildings in your town—post office, churches, stores, barber shop, town hall, library, schools, firehouse. Your local library or historical society might have pictures of the way your town looked earlier in the century. Show the pictures and ask the participants if they recognize any of the buildings. Ask if anyone has a special memory to share with the group, something that happened to them in connection with one of the buildings.

2. **Religion**. Invite a retired minister or rabbi to come and share memories about religious life in your town. Ask the participants to share their earliest memories of the town's Sabbath observances, religious holidays, visiting preachers, revival meetings, prayer meetings, Ladies Aid Society, Sunday School, Bible School, prayer and Bible reading in school. Ask if religious life was important in the community.

3. **Radio**. Play excerpts of old radio shows about small town life, such as "Vic and Sade," "Life of Riley," "The Great Gildersleeve," and "Fibber McGee and Molly." You could have the participants guess the name of the show or just play short sections for their enjoyment. Ask them if the shows accurately portrayed small town life.

4. **Radio**. If you are a fan of Garrison Keillor's "Prairie Home Companion" tell the participants about Lake Wobegon. Tapes and records are available from Minnesota Public Radio (45 East Eighth Street, St. Paul, Minnesota 55101). You could play excerpts from the show, particularly the monologs and the "commercials."

5. **Birthplaces**. If you have a diverse population of people from all over the country (or the world), ask each participant to tell where she/he is from and a little bit about the place where she/he grew up. You could get a map of the United States (or the world), and put labels (with names on them) where each participant was born.

6. **History**. Invite a member of the local historical society (one of your participants may be one!) to come and talk, informally, about the history of your town and how it has changed over the years. You may have a participant who has an exceptional memory for people and where they lived.

7. **Music**. Ask the participants to name songs that have names of cities in their titles. If your group likes to sing, you could sing some of them. You could also play "Name That Tune" with these songs.

8. **Song Title Quiz.**

>   I left my heart in. . .**San Francisco**
>
>   "East Side, West Side" is about which city?   **New York**
>
>   I've got a gal in. . .**Kalamazoo**
>
>   Give my regards to. . .**Broadway**
>
>   What city has a choo-choo named for it?   **Chattanooga**
>
>   I love. . .**Paris**
>
>   What is "my city of dreams"?   **Vienna**
>
>   Moon over. . .**Miami**

Down Memory Lane

Hard-hearted Hannah is the vamp of which city? **Savannah**

It's a long, long way to. . .**Tipperary**

Where are the white cliffs? **Dover, England**

Arrivederci. . .**Roma**

How are things in. . .**Glocca Morra**

April in. . .**Paris**

What is that "toddlin'" town? **Chicago**

9. **Related Activity**. Invite a local barbershop quartet to sing a few old songs for the participants.

10. **Related Activity**. Invite a local high school band to perform. The participants could tell the students what your town was like when they were young.

11. **Related Activity**. If it's summertime, make hand-cranked ice cream or hand-squeezed lemonade as a group. (Some towns saved their ice from the winter in ice houses and made ice cream for everyone in the summer.) If it's winter, make apple pies.

12. **Related Activity**. Show the movie "Our Town," based on the play by Thornton Wilder. If your group likes drama, read part or all of the original play and talk about its portrayal of small town life.

DISCUSSION

Ask the participants to share their memories about the following aspects of small town life:

Parades - when did they have them, who was in them
Celebrating the 4th of July and/or Memorial Day - ceremonies, fireworks (Sing patriotic songs.)
Volunteer fire department
Bells - town hall, school, firehouse, churches
Mail delivery
Election day
Soda fountain, ice cream parlors, and other meeting places for the younger generation
Travelling salesmen
Leisure time activities, such as dances, movies, swimming, fishing, band concerts, boating
Telephone service - party lines, ringing the operator to make calls
Travelling cultural shows (such as Chautauqua) or vaudeville shows or stars
Stores in the town
Town sports - baseball, football, softball
Neighbors helping other neighbors
Quilting bees
Town doctors, quarantines, midwives, hospitals
A shared event of great importance...natural disasters, major celebrations, etc.

You could end the session by (1) singing "Dear Hearts and Gentle People" or another song that might have special meaning to your city or state, (2) giving each person a picture of the town, and/or (3) serving lemonade and homemade cookies, simple ice cream sundaes, or apple pie.

NEEDLEWORK

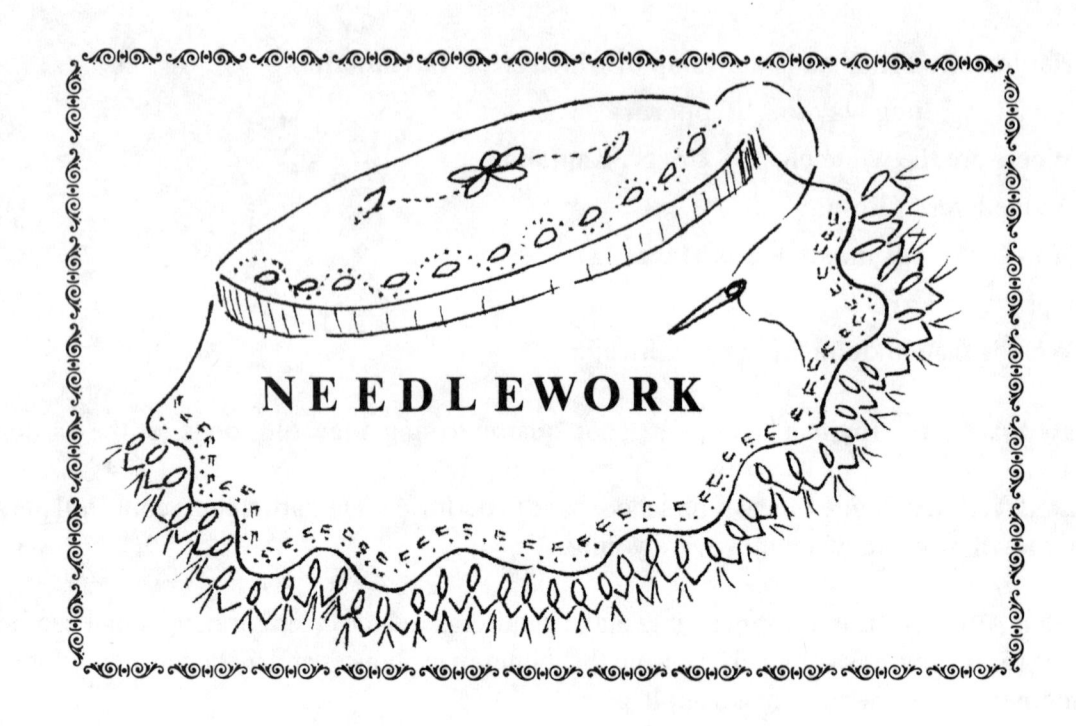

IN THE MOOD

Music Possibilities

1. Recordings of pre-1940 bluegrass, country, or folk music.

2. Recordings of parlor music, like a piano playing pre-1940 popular music.

Visual Possibilities

1. Sayings to post on the wall:
    "A stitch in time saves nine."
    "Like finding a needle in a haystack."
    "You can't make a silk purse out of a sow's ear."
    "You have me in stitches."

2. Find all the handmade needlework you can, to hang up or to display on a table (particularly if made by residents). The older the work, the better. Could be sewing, crochet, knitting, embroidery, quilting, patchwork, applique, needlepoint, tatting.

3. Display table of notions. See Activity #4 for suggestions.

ACTIVITIES

1. **Theme Song**. A good song to sing or play right before the session begins is "Aunt Dinah's Quilting Party."

2. **Sharing Needlework**. Pass around all the needlework you have gathered for display. With the participants' needlework, ask them to tell how it was made, what materials were used, and how long it took to make. With the other pieces, tell something about each piece and encourage the participants to share their reactions, memories, etc.

3. **Speaker**. Invite a local teacher or artist of quilting, embroidery, knitting, tatting, needlepoint, etc., to share her/his fabric art with the participants and to talk about the pieces. Encourage the participants to ask questions and to share their own experiences.

4. **Notions**. Ask the participants to describe the use of some of the following objects: (Show the object, or a picture of it, if you can.)

> seam ripper - cuts the thread in a seam
> bobbin - holds thread inside a sewing machine
> darning needle - large needle used in repairing holes
> pinking shears - scissors that cut in a zigzag pattern
> tape measure - 60" flexible measurer
> tracing wheel - marks patterns onto carbon paper
> hem gauge - small ruler with a moveable pointer
> zipper, button, hook and eye, snaps - used to hold garments together
> thimble - cap for finger, to protect it from a needle
> crochet hook - used to crochet
> rickrack - zigzag trim
> knitting needles - used for knitting
> elastic - stretch tape, used for gathering fabric
> pin cushion - holds pins
> dress shield - protects garments from perspiration
> dressmaker's carbon paper - for marking pattern onto fabric
> crochet cotton - thread for crochetting
> dress form - a body mold for fitting garments
> embroidery floss - thick thread for embroidery
> emery bag - for sharpening needles
> buttonhole scissors - shaped to cut buttonholes easily
> embroidery hoop - for holding fabric taut
> tailor tacker - used to mark fabric
> shoulder pads - used to give shape to shoulders
> point turner - tool used to push out corners of garments
> beeswax - used to rub on thread to prevent knots

Notions that may be difficult to locate:
> egg darner - egg-shaped wood with a handle used as backing when darning socks
> plaiting machine - for making hand-made trimmings
> corset clasps - strip with hooks and eyes for sewing into a corset
> featherbone - quills covered with cotton for distending skirt ruffles, etc.
> stilleto or awl - pointed tool used to pierce holes in fabric
> bodkin - an over-sized blunt needle with a large eye for drawing ribbon or elastic through a loop, hem, or casing

5. **Sewing Machines**. Ask the participants what kind of sewing machines they owned and what features were on them. (Common types: Singer, Pfaff, Brother, White, Kenmore. Types no longer made: Burdick, New Queen.) Ask the participants to share their memories of using treadle machines. (Someone associated with the nursing home might have a treadle machine you could borrow.) If you own a newer sewing machine with many features, especially an electronic one, give a brief demonstration.

6. **Types of Fabric**. Show samples of various types of fabric and ask the participants if they remember what kind it is and if they ever made or wore anything from that kind of fabric. Examples: calico, corduroy, wool, silk, linen, muslin, gabardine, velvet, kettlecloth.

7. **Related Activity.** Some groups might be able to make a simple quilt as a long-term project. The nine-patch or the puffed block would be simple ones to piece and the quilt could be knotted together. Or some participants could make some small knitted or crochetted blocks to sew together for a blanket.

8. **Related Activity**. If you have the space, invite a local quilting or needlework guild to have a "show" at your facility. Some of the residents might help as hostesses or with serving refreshments.

DISCUSSION

1. Can some of you share your earliest memory of learning how to sew or do other needlework? What kind of needlework was it and who taught you? Did you like it? Did any of you make samplers?

2. Can some of you share what kinds of needlework you did as adults? Was it something you did every spare minute or just occasionally, as a hobby?

3. Did any of you ever give your needlework as gifts? Did any of you ever do needlework that was given away for a charitable cause? Tell us about it.

4. Can anyone remember having a favorite dress, blouse, shirt, or other garment? What made it special?

5. Have any of you ever taken part in a quilting bee? What do you remember about it? Can you remember how to put a quilt on a quilting frame?

6. Did any of you ever win any prizes for your needlework? Tell us about it.

7. Did any of you ever teach your skills to someone else? Who?

To end the session, you could read this quote from a pioneer woman: "We women made those quilts as fast as we could so our families wouldn't freeze and as beautiful as we could so our hearts wouldn't break."

IN THE MOOD

Music Possibilities

1. Songs about news and talking:

   "The Telephone Hour" (from "Bye Bye Birdie")
   "Pick a Little, Talk a Little" (from "The Music Man")
   "Please Don't Talk About Me When I'm Gone"
   "People Will Say We're In Love" (from "Oklahoma")
   "I Talk to the Trees" (from "Paint Your Wagon")
   "Happy Talk" (from "South Pacific")
   "It's the Talk of the Town"
   "Small Talk" (from "The Pajama Game")

2. Recording of Lowell Thomas, Edward R. Murrow, or Walter Winchell giving the news, available on collections of vintage radio broadcasts. (See Appendix A.)

Visual Possibilities

1. On a poster, use this quote from Will Rogers, "All I know is what I read in the papers."

2. The front page of all the different newspapers you can find: local papers, nearby city paper, "New York Times," "USA Today," news magazines, college papers, tabloids, *People*, *Life* magazine.

3. On posters on the wall, put the call letters of all the local television or radio stations that broadcast the news.

4. Pictures of famous news people, such as the following: Lowell Thomas, Edward R. Murrow, Walter Winchell, Walter Cronkite, Huntley and Brinkley, Dave Garroway, Hedda Hopper, H.L. Mencken, Louella Parsons. See list under Activity #7. (Vestal Press has a good photo book called *Great Radio Personalities in Historic Photographs*. There is a book from Dover Publications called *Great News Photos and the Stories Behind Them*.)

5. A picture or a facsimile of one of the early radio microphones.

ACTIVITIES

1. **Radio**. If you have found a recording of some old news broadcasts, play excerpts for the participants. You could (1) play the excerpt and have the participants figure out the event, or (2) name the event excerpted, play it, and then ask the participants if they remember when they first heard it and what their reaction to it was.

2. **Film**. Check your local library film service and see if they have any old newsreels that you could borrow. You could ask the same questions from Activity #1.

3. **News Stories**. Ask the participants if they remember what they were doing and how they heard about these momentous news stories:

>The end of World War I, 1918
>The death of President Harding, 1923
>Lindbergh's solo flight to France, 1927
>Stock Market crash, October 1929
>Kidnapping of Lindbergh's baby, 1932
>Bombing of Pearl Harbor, December 1941
>D-Day, the Normandy Invasion, June 1944
>The death of President Franklin Roosevelt, 1945
>End of World War II - VE Day in May 1945 and VJ Day in August 1945
>The dropping of the first atomic bomb, August 1945
>The launching of the first Sputnik, 1957
>The assassination of President Kennedy, 1963

4. **Newspapers**. Ask the participants to name their hometown newspapers and any others to which they may have subscribed. Many newspapers have a regular feature that reports news headlines from 5, 10, and 25 years ago. If yours does, read some recent ones and ask the participants if they remember the news event. Ask if any ever worked on a newspaper and, if so, what it was like.

5. **Advice Columns**. Save some of the more interesting "Dear Abby" or "Ann Landers" columns. (Each have books out, too.) Read the questions to the participants and encourage them to give their advice. After a short discussion, read the advice given in the column. This is a good opportunity to compare changes in attitudes to morality and customs. If you can find a humorous one, it is also a good way to end a session with a laugh!

6. **Tabloids**. Ask if any ever read the tabloid newspapers and if so, which ones? If you can obtain a copy of the "National Enquirer" or "The Star," read aloud some short, interesting stories from these. Ask the participants if they remember some of these stories that were sensationalized by the tabloids:

> Leopold-Loeb murder case
> Story of Peaches and Daddy
> Kidnapping of Aimee Semple McPherson
> Murder of movie director William Desmond Taylor

7. **Personalities**. Ask if any can remember these news people and for what they were known:

Floyd Gibbons - first newsman on the radio in the 1920s; wore an eye patch; had a rapid-fire style of delivery; hosted a radio show called "Headline Hunters"

H.V. Kaltenborn - "dean" of radio news commentators and one of the earliest on the air

Mary Margaret McBride - newspaperwoman; "first lady of radio"; had a long-running radio talk show

Walter Winchell - newscaster on the radio, hosting "Walter Winchell's Journal"; began his news broadcast by saying, "To Mr. and Mrs. North America and All Ships at Sea"

Westbrook Pegler - newspaper columnist

Heywood Broun - newspaper columnist

Cesar Saerchinger - radio show, "Story Behind the Headlines"

H.L. Mencken - news journalist

Dave Garroway - first host of the "Today Show"

J. Fred Muggs - first animal--a chimpanzee--on a news program, "Today Show"

Graham McNamee - 1920s and 1930s radio newsman; reporter and announcer with a deep voice

Edwin C. Hill - gave "the human side of the news"

Louella Parsons ("Hollywood Hotel") and Hedda Hopper - Hollywood gossip columnists on the radio (Presta Sounds has a tape of Louella Parsons.)

Albert Mitchell - "The Answer Man"

Drew Pearson - wrote *The Washington Merry-Go-Round*

Edward R. Murrow - radio and television investigative reporter; television shows called "See It Now" and "Person to Person"

Lowell Thomas - news commentator, writer, producer

Gabriel Heatter - radio reporter and commentator; host of "We the People"; started his broadcasts by saying, "Ah yes, there's good news tonight."

Bill Stern - sports annnouncer (Presta Sounds has a tape of his show.)

Ben Grauer - NBC commentator and reporter; covered major news events

8. **Personals**. Many people meet other people through the Personals section of a newspaper. Ask the participants if any of them ever put a notice in the personals column and what the results were. Read some current "Personals" ads from your local newspaper. You could then ask two or three participants to volunteer to have the group help them write an ad as if she/he were looking for a date.

9. **Related Activity**. Show a film about the newspaper business. Suggestions: "The Front Page" (there are two versions), "His Gal Friday," "The Philadelphia Story," "Woman of the Year."

DISCUSSION

1. Have any of you ever gotten your name in the paper? Do you remember why? How about your picture in the paper?

2. Do you remember any news stories that were so important that you read and listened to everything you could?

3. Did any of you see newsreels? Where did you see them? How often where they available?

4. Have any of you ever written a letter to the editor of a newspaper? Do you remember what you wrote?

5. Who is your favorite columnist or news anchor today?

If you can find a humorous news event in your local paper, use it to end the session. Your library or bookstore might have a collection of odd news stories. Also, some newspapers publish a special section of Valentine messages each February 14, some of which are very funny.

This is a big topic and could provide programs for several sessions, perhaps on different themes (especially if you can find appropriate recordings), such as comedies, musical/variety, soap operas, westerns, mysteries, etc.

IN THE MOOD

Music Possibilities

1. Recorded music that was popular on the radio. Examples:

    Big Band music...Benny Goodman, Jimmy Dorsey, Les Brown, Glenn Miller. (In the 1940s, there were programs called "Cavalcade of Popular Bands" sponsored by Coca-Cola and "Hit Parade" sponsored by Lucky Strike Tobacco.)

    Favorite singers - Rudy Vallee, Bing Crosby, Frank Sinatra, Kate Smith, Gene Autry, Dinah Shore, Sons of the Pioneers, Mills Brothers, Mildred Bailey, Ben Bernie, Russ Columbo.

2. Theme songs from radio programs. (See Activity #2.)

3. An orchestra made famous by radio...Longines Symphony, NBC Orchestra with Toscanini, Voice of Firestone Orchestra.

Visual Possibilities

1. Have an old radio set in the room or a picture of one or have a picture of someone listening to a radio or an old crystal radio set.

2. Pictures of radio personalities. (You can often find pictures of radio singers on the covers of old piano music. See also Vestal Press' *Great Radio Personalities in Historic Photographs*.)

ACTIVITIES

1. **Pictures**. If you are able to find pictures of several radio personalities, pass them around. Ask the participants who is in the picture and to share anything they remember about the person and their work on the radio. If you can find them, show "then and now" pictures.

2. **Theme Songs**. Play theme songs, if you can find recordings of them, and see if the participants remember whose they were. If you can't find theme song recordings, name the theme song and ask whose it was. Here are some suggestions:

   "Thanks For the Memory" - **Bob Hope**
   "Where the Blue Of the Night Meets the Gold Of the Day" - **Bing Crosby**
   "This is My Lucky Day" - **Lucky Strike Hit Parade,** begun in 1935
   "Blue Moon" - **Louella Parsons' "Hollywood Hotel"**
   "Ida" - **Eddie Cantor** (Eddie's wife's name was Ida.)
   "When the Moon Comes Over the Mountain" - **Kate Smith**
   "Back In the Saddle Again" - **Gene Autry**. (His show was "The Melody Ranch Gang Show.")
   "William Tell Overture" - **Lone Ranger**, started in 1933
   "Love in Bloom" - **Jack Benny**, started in 1933
   "Campbells are Coming" - **Camel Caravan Show, with Benny Goodman**
   "Thinking of You" - **Kay Kyser's "Kollege of Musical Knowledge"**
   "The Flight of the Bumblebee" - **Green Hornet**
   "One of Those Songs" - **Jimmy Durante**
   "Your Time Is My Time" - **Rudy Vallee** (on his show "The Fleishman Hour")
   "Red River Valley" - **"Our Gal Sunday"**
   Sound of a squeaky door - **"Inner Sanctum"**
   Clock striking midnight - **"Captain Midnight"**
   "Carolina Moon" - **Morton Downey, tenor**
   "Smile, Darn Ya, Smile" - **Fred Allen**

3. **Introductions**. Play recordings of introductions to shows, or read them yourself, and see if the residents can guess the show.

   "Good evening, Mr. and Mrs. America." - **Walter Winchell**
   "Who knows what evil lurks in the hearts of men." - **"The Shadow"**
   "Wake up, America—time to stump the experts!" - **"Information Please"**
   "Faster than a speeding bullet" - **Superman**
   "Get this and get it straight, crime is a sucker's road and those who travel it wind up in the gutter, the prison, or an early grave." - **"The Adventures of Philip Marlowe"**
   "Can this girl from a mining town in the West find happiness as the wife of a wealthy and titled Englishman?" - **"Our Gal Sunday"**
   "The sweetest music this side of heaven" - **Guy Lombardo**
   "Heigh-ho, everybody." - **Rudy Vallee**
   "Return with us now to those thrilling days of yesteryear! From out of the past comes the thundering hoofbeats of the great horse Silver!" - **The Lone Ranger**
   Famous sign-off: "Good-night, Mrs. Calabash, wherever you are." - **Jimmy Durante**

74 *Down Memory Lane*

4. **Excerpts**. Play short excerpts (taped, if possible) from several old radio shows and see if the participants can identify the show and/or the performers. Try to stimulate discussion after each excerpt by asking some of these questions:

>   Who was the performer?
>   What show?
>   When was the show on?
>   Did you or anyone in your family listen to it regularly?
>   Do you remember anyone else from the show?
>   What was the show about? (if it was a situation show)

5. **Characters**. Ask the participants what they remember about these characters or personalities:

>   Original Texaco Fire Chief - **Ed Wynn**
>   Fibber McGee and Molly - **had an over-stuffed closet**
>   Red Godfrey, the Warbling Banjoist" - **Arthur Godfrey**
>   Titus Moody, Mrs. Nussbaum, Ajax Cassidy, Senator Claghorn - **"Allen's Alley" (Fred Allen)**
>   Rochester - **worked for Jack Benny**
>   Richigan Fishigan of Shishigan, Michigan - **on "Vic and Sade"**
>   U.S. Captain Albright - **Captain Midnight**
>   Archie - **Manager of "Duffy's Tavern" who said "Where the elite meet to eat"**
>   The All American Boy" - **Jack Armstrong**
>   Mortimer Snerd - **Edgar Bergen's dummy**
>   Jerry Colonna - **comedian on Bob Hope's show**
>   Tonto - **the Lone Ranger's friend**
>   Nick and Nora Charles - **detective couple on "The Thin Man"**
>   Kingfish - **character on "Amos 'n Andy"**
>   Baby Snooks - **Fanny Brice juvenile character**

6. **Radio Today**. The first radios were crystal sets, needing ear phones to hear. Show and talk about the Walkman radios used by joggers. Tell the participants about local stations that are now rebroadcasting old radio shows and when the programs are on the air.

7. **The Family Radio**. If you listened to Garrison Keillor's "Prairie Home Companion," a live radio show broadcast on public radio stations Saturday nights, tell the participants about it. Play a recording of "The Family Radio," a song about this topic. The song is on an album of the same name, which is available from Minnesota Public Radio, 45 East 8th Street, St. Paul, Minnesota 55101.

DISCUSSION

1. What is your earliest memory of the radio?

2. During what part of your life did you listen to the radio the most?

3. Name some of the old shows you remember. Who were your favorite performers or shows?

Down Memory Lane 75

4. Did any of you have a crystal set with earphones? Did any of you ever make a crystal radio?

5. Did any of you have a favorite night to listen to the radio? When did you usually turn it on? Was the radio on all the time or just for favorite programs?

6. If you lived in the country, could you get stations easily or only at night?

7. Do you remember any local radio personalities?

8. Did any of you hear about Pearl Harbor on the radio? Did any of you listen to the Grand Ole Opry? Did you ever dance at home to the "Make Believe Ballroom"? Did any of you hear the famous "War of the Worlds" broadcast, October 30, 1938? Did any of you listen to the Fireside Chats? Were any of you regular listeners to the Metropolitan Opera Broadcasts on Saturday afternoons? Tell us what you remember.

For more specific information about radio programs, consult these books: *Memories, Dreams and Thoughts* (see Appendix A); trivia books; library books about the early days of radio. Appendix A also lists several companies that sell vintage radio programs.

You could end the session by playing an excerpt from a radio comedy show.

OPERA

This topic will not be for every group but there are places where this would be a very popular subject. If your group knows very little about opera but is receptive to hearing this music and learning more about it, you could approach this session more as music appreciation than as reminiscence. Ask the group!

IN THE MOOD

Music Possibilities

1. Play a popular, well-known opera, such as "La Boheme," "La Traviata," or "Madame Butterfly." A recording that has excerpts rather than the entire opera would probably be more "listenable."

2. There are recordings (owned by many libraries) available of collections of arias sung by different opera stars of the 1920s, 1930s, and 1940s.

Visual Possibilities

1. Check your library for books that have pictures of opera stars of the past and scenes from well-known operas. Display the pictures or give a copy to each person who attends.

2. Have a table display of objects: books about opera, opera scores, staff paper, baton, metronome, record jackets from opera recordings.

ACTIVITIES

1. **Local Opera**. If you live in a city that has an opera company, invite someone from the company to talk to the participants about behind-the-scenes details and anecdotes of staging an opera.

2. **Opera Excerpts**. If you have been able to find a collection of arias from several operas, play excerpts and ask the participants if they remember which opera they are from. Look for recordings by opera stars of the past. Here are some suggestions of well-known melodies from operas:

> Mascagni's "Cavalleria Rusticana" - "Intermezzo"
> Puccini's "La Boheme" - "Mi chiamano Mimi" or "Quando me'n vo'soletta" ("Musetta's Waltz")
> Bizet's "Carmen" - "L'amour est un oiseau rebelle" or "Toreador Song"
> Offenbach's "The Tales of Hoffman" - the Overture
> Wagner's "Lohengrin" - "The Wedding Chorus" ("Treulich gefuhrt")
> Donizetti's "Lucia di Lammermoor" - Sextet at the end of Act 2 ("Chi mi frena in tal momento?")
> Puccini's "Madama Butterfly" - "Un bel di"
> Verdi's "La Traviata" - "Libiamo, libiamo, ne' lieti calici"
> Wagner's "Tristan und Isolde" - "Prelude"
> Verdi's "Rigoletto" - "La Donna e Mobile"
> Verdi's "Aida" - "Celeste Aida"
> Donizetti's "L'Elisir d'Amore" - "Quanto e bella"
> Johann Strauss' "Die Fledermaus" - "The Champagne Chorus"
> Verdi's "Otello" - Duet in first act - "Gia nella notta densa"

3. **Opera Stars**. If you have been able to find pictures of opera stars of the past, show these and see if the participants recognize them. If you have no pictures, name the following stars and see if the participants remember who they were, if they ever saw them perform, or any other information they might know about each.

> Enrico Caruso, most famous tenor of the early 20th century
> Eleanor Steber, soprano
> Robert Merrill, tenor
> Mario Lanza, tenor, more involved in Hollywood than in the opera stage
> Maria Callas, Greek soprano
> John McCormack, Irish tenor
> Amelita Galli-Curci, coloratura soprano
> Ezio Pinza, bass, starred at the Met, as well as in the stage musical "South Pacific"
> Lily Pons, soprano
> Lawrence Tibbett, baritone, sang frequently on the radio as well as on the stage
> Lauritz Melchior, tenor
> John Charles Thomas, baritone, he always ended his radio show by saying "Good night, mother"
> Rosa Ponselle, mezzo-soprano
> Kirsten Flagstad, Wagnerian soprano
> Lotte Lehmann, soprano
> Grace Moore, soprano, starred at the Met, in movies, and on Broadway
> Paul Robeson, bass, famed for singing "Ol' Man River," was also an actor and an athlete
> Marion Anderson, she gave an historic concert at the Lincoln Memorial in Washington, D.C., in 1939, and was the first black person to sing at the Metropolitan Opera
> Feodor Chaliapin, Russian bass
> Lucrezia Bori, soprano
> Jan Peerce, tenor, sang frequently on the radio, especially with the NBC Symphony
> Gladys Swarthout, sang opera on the radio as well as on the stage

4. **Opera props.** Show or name an item, asking with which opera it is associated and how this prop fits into the plot.

    Mask - **"Un Ballo in Maschera" ("The Masked Ball")**
    Crutch - **"Amahl and the Night Visitors"**
    Barber scissors and comb - **"The Barber of Seville"**
    Hand fan and castanets - **"Carmen"**
    Candle, a key, and a bonnet - **"La Boheme"**
    Clown (use a picture or a doll) - **"Pagliacci"**
    Burlap bag - **"Rigoletto"**
    Ring - **"Der Ring des Nibelungen"**
    Swan (picture or figurine) - **"Lohengrin"**

5. **Opera plots.**

    What opera takes place in Egypt?
        "Aida" by Verdi
    "La Donna e Mobile" means "The Woman is Fickle" and is sung in what opera?
        "Rigoletto" by Verdi
    In what Italian opera does a Japanese girl have a love affair with an American naval officer?
        "Madama Butterfly" by Puccini
    What opera was the first one written for television and had its premiere in 1951?
        "Amahl and the Night Visitors" by Menotti
    In what opera does the hero remember the three loves of his life while drinking in a tavern?
        "Tales of Hoffman" by Offenbach
    In what opera does the finale take place outside a bullfighting arena?
        "Carmen" by Bizet
    What opera is about a love potion?
        "L'Elisir D'Amore" or "The Elixir of Love" by Donizetti
    What opera, by Beethoven, takes place in a dungeon?
        "Fidelio"
    What opera, based on a folk tale, is about two children who get lost in the woods?
        "Hansel and Gretel" by Humperdinck
    In what opera does the heroine throw herself from a building at the end?
        "Tosca" by Verdi
    What opera is about "The Lady of the Camellias"?
        "La Traviata" by Verdi
    Who were Wagner's most famous lovers?
        Tristan and Isolde
    What was the first American jazz opera?
        "Porgy and Bess" by George Gershwin
    What opera is about a group of cold, starving artists?
        "La Boheme" by Puccini
    At the conclusion of what opera are the lovers buried alive?
        "Aida" by Verdi
    In what opera does the heroine go mad after killing the bridegroom?
        "Lucia di Lammermoor" by Donizetti

6. **Humor.** To add a little humor to this session, see if your library has the book *Great Operatic Disasters* by Hugh Vickers, 1979, St. Martin's Press, Inc., New York. It is anecdotal so you could read short excerpts.

7. **Related Activity.** Show the movie "The Great Caruso."

8. **Related Activity.** There are biographies available about opera stars. If you have a reading group, read one of these books. Robert Merrill and Beverly Sills have written very entertaining ones.

DISCUSSION

1. Can any of you remember the first opera music you ever heard? What opera? Do you remember who was singing? Did you hear it live or on the radio?

2. What operas have any of you seen live? Can you tell us what you remember about it?

3. Have any of you listened to the Metropolitan Opera radio broadcasts on Saturday afternoon? Do any of you remember the name of the announcer of these broadcasts for 40 years? (Milton Cross)

4. Did any of you listen to early recordings by opera stars, such as Caruso, on the gramophone?

5. Do any of you remember sending donations to save the Metropolitan Opera when it was in financial trouble in the 1930s?

6. Have any of you ever been to hear an opera at the old Metropolitan Opera House? What was it like there? Did any of you ever stand in the Standing Room Only section? Do you remember what it cost? Have any of you ever used opera glasses?

7. Have you ever been involved in the production of an opera? What do you remember about it?

8. Were any of you ever inspired to take singing lessons because of opera? Tell us about it.

OPERETTA

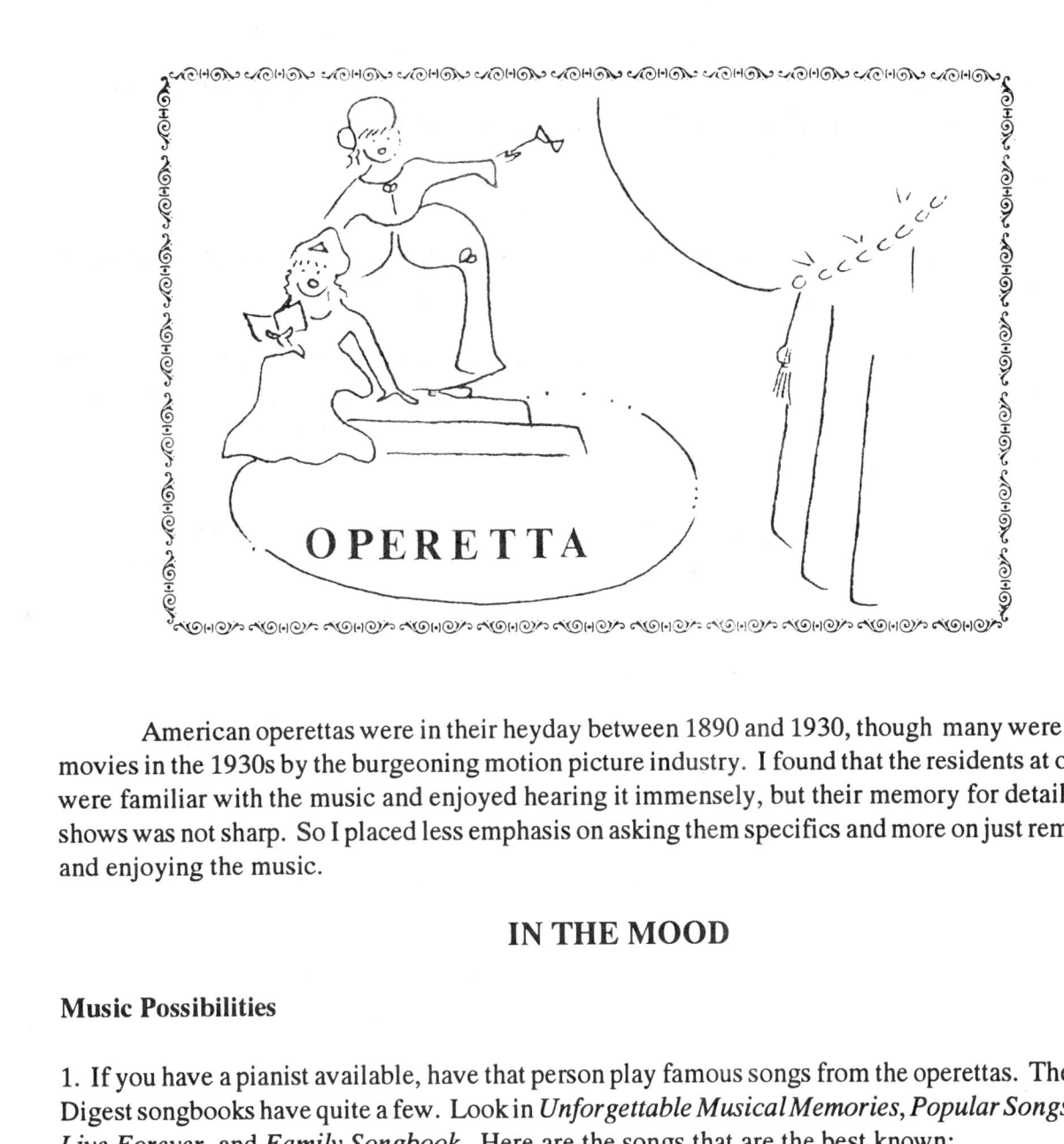

American operettas were in their heyday between 1890 and 1930, though many were made into movies in the 1930s by the burgeoning motion picture industry. I found that the residents at our facility were familiar with the music and enjoyed hearing it immensely, but their memory for detail about the shows was not sharp. So I placed less emphasis on asking them specifics and more on just remembering and enjoying the music.

IN THE MOOD

Music Possibilities

1. If you have a pianist available, have that person play famous songs from the operettas. The Reader's Digest songbooks have quite a few. Look in *Unforgettable Musical Memories, Popular Songs That Will Live Forever*, and *Family Songbook*. Here are the songs that are the best known:

"Will You Remember" ("Sweetheart")	"Kiss Me Again"
"Ah, Sweet Mystery of Life"	"Gypsy Love Song"
"March of the Toys"	"A Kiss in the Dark"
"Softly, As in a Morning Sunrise"	"My Hero"
"Indian Love Call"	"Rose-Marie"
"Lover, Come Back To Me"	"One Alone"
"One Kiss"	"Yours is My Heart Alone"
"The Desert Song"	"Song of the Vagabonds"
"Stout-hearted Men"	"Serenade" from "The Student Prince"

2. Play the soundtrack from one of the better-known American operettas, such as the following: "The New Moon," "The Vagabond King," "The Desert Song," "The Student Prince," "Babes In Toyland," "Mlle. Modeste," "Naughty Marietta," "Rose-Marie," "Blossom Time," "May Wine," "The Blue Paradise," "Maytime."

3. Your library may have recordings of famous singers performing songs from the operettas. Look for records by Mario Lanza, Nelson Eddy, Jeanette MacDonald, Dennis Morgan.

Visual Possibilities

1. Scenes from operettas and pictures of people asssociated with operettas in the early part of this century: Victor Herbert, Rudolf Friml, Sigmund Romberg, Oscar Hammerstein II.

2. Pictures of the stars who appeared in operettas, both on the stage and in the movies: Jeanette MacDonald and Nelson Eddy (a movie poster might be available), Emma Trentini, Dennis King, Fritzi Scheff, Brian Hooker, Rida Johnson Young, Rise Stevens, Richard Tauber, Evelyn Herbert, John Boles, Carlotta King, Howard Keel, Irene Manning.

3. Posters: Write the names of the operettas listed under Music Possibilities on large posters for display in the activity room. Have a large sign reading "Broadway." Display old sheet music if you have it.

ACTIVITIES

1. **To Begin**. Ask the participants to name all the operettas they can remember—British, American, and Viennese.

2. **Songs**. Play some of the songs listed under Music Possibilities and see if the participants can remember anything about them. Ask questions such as these: Can you remember the name of the song or of the operetta? Do you remember seeing it? Did you see it on the stage or in the movies?

3. **Photographs**. Share any relevant photographs you have found with the participants. Ask if they can identify the person or the show or if they remember anything about the person or the show after you identify them.

4. **Operetta Trivia.**

> Who composed "Ah, Sweet Mystery of Life"?
> **Victor Herbert**
>
> "The March of the Wooden Soldiers" is in what operetta?
> **"Babes in Toyland" by Victor Herbert**
>
> The chorus of what song starts "When I'm calling you-oooo-oooo"?
> **"Indian Love Call" from "Rose-Marie"**
>
> What song from "Mlle. Modeste" by Victor Herbert was Fritzi Scheff's theme song?
> **"Kiss Me Again"**
>
> What two movie operetta stars were known as "America's Singing Sweethearts"?
> **Jeanette MacDonald and Nelson Eddy**

What song, from the operetta "The New Moon," is sung to rally a chorus of men to a mutiny on their ship?
"Stout-hearted Men"

What operetta was the first one that was made into an all-talking, all-singing 1929 movie starring John Boles and Carlotta King? (It was set in old French Morocco.)
"The Desert Song"

What operetta's hero was a French beggar-poet named Francois Villon? (It was based on the play "If I Were King.")
"The Vagabond King"

What operetta was about the Canadian Mounties?
"Rose-Marie"

What two men wrote the best-known British operettas?
Gilbert and Sullivan

5. **Related Activity**. Show a movie that was based on an operetta. Possibilities: "New Moon," "Vagabond King," "The Desert Song," "Naughty Marietta," "Rose-Marie," "The Pirates of Penzance."

6. **Related Activity**. If you have a singer and an accompanist available, ask them to do a concert of operetta music. It would be more interesting if you could tell something about each song or operetta in addition to the music. If you have access to the Reader's Digest songbooks, there is information given before each song. Ask the participants if any of these songs were particular favorites or what memories were associated with them.

DISCUSSION

1. Did any of you ever attend a tour concert by Sigmund Romberg and his Orchestra? Can you tell us about it?

2. Did any of you ever attend a live performance of an operetta? What do you remember about it?

3. How many of you remember seeing one of the operettas as a movie by Nelson Eddy and Jeanette MacDonald? Do you remember which ones? Which was better, the play or the movie?

4. Have any of you ever been a part of putting on an operetta? Tell us about it.

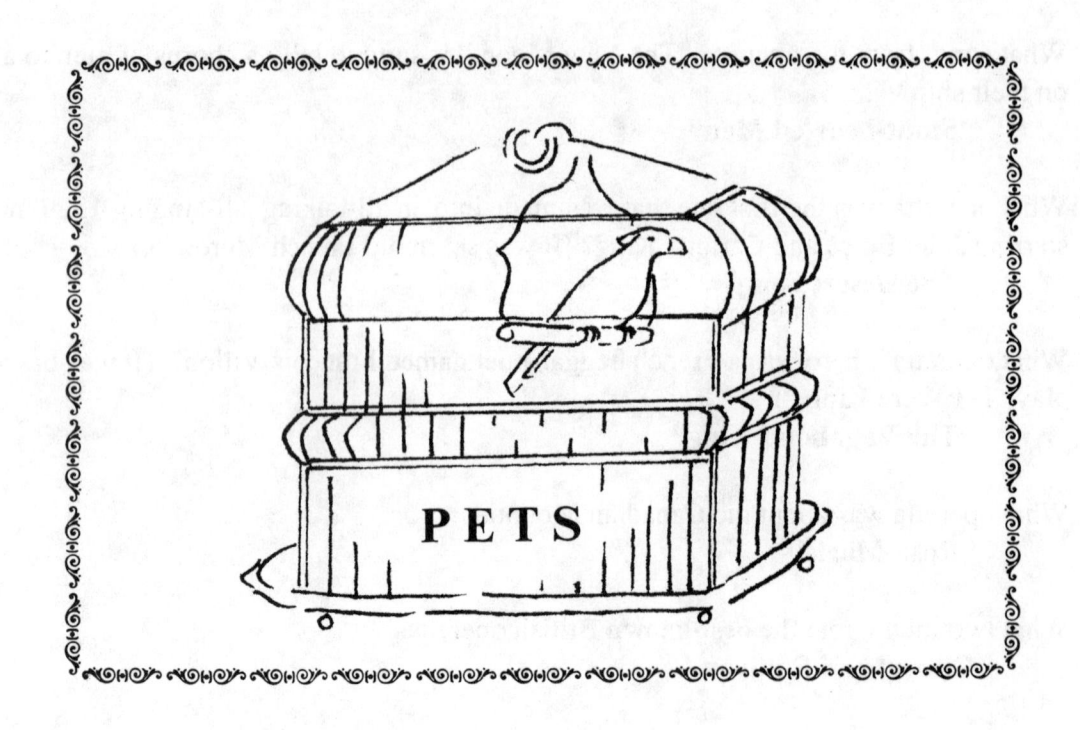

IN THE MOOD

Music Possibilities

1. Songs about animals:

    "Where, Oh Where, Has My Little Dog Gone?"
    "How Much Is That Doggie In the Window?"
    "I Had a Cat and My Cat Pleased Me"
    "Talk to the Animals" (from the movie "Dr. Doolittle")
    Theme from "The Pink Panther"
    "Bye, Bye Blackbird"
    "Let's All Sing Like the Birdies Sing"
    "Glow-Worm"
    "Animal Crackers In My Soup" (Sung by Shirley Temple)
    "Donkey Serenade" (Sung by Allen Jones)

2. Folk music records, particularly Pete Seeger's "Birds, Beasts, Bugs, and Little Fishes." (Look in the children's section of the library, or write to Folkways Records, 632 Broadway, New York, New York 10012.)

Visual Possibilities

Pictures of animals. Cats or dogs are the easiest to find, but look for some exotic animals, too, like pandas and koalas. (There may be staff or family members that collect pictures of certain kinds of animals that you could borrow.)

ACTIVITIES

1. **Former Pets**. Ask each participant who had a pet in the past to share his or her experiences with the group: the pet's name, what kind of animal, and the funniest or most interesting thing the animal ever did.

2. **New Pets**. This is a good session for inviting family members or staff to bring in their pets to share with the participants. (In order to have time for the participants to share their experiences, you might limit the number of pets that are brought.) People love to talk about their pets, so you can ask each pet-owner to show off the animal and to tell some of the funny or interesting things that their pet has done.

3. **Animal Groups**. Ask the participants to complete these phrases:

A herd of...elephants	A bevy of...swans or quail
A clutch of...chicks	A colony of...ants
A flight of...birds	A flock of...sheep or geese
A gaggle of...geese	A hive of...bees
A litter of...pigs, cats, or dogs	A pack of...hounds or wolves
A pride of...lions	A school of...fish
A swarm of...bees	A team of...horses or ducks
A tribe of...monkeys	A yoke of...oxen

4. **Animal Babies**. Give the name of an animal and ask the participants what the young are called. Some of the participants (especially if they lived on a farm) may have other names for some of these.

bear...cub	horse...colt, filly, foal
cat...kitten	kangaroo...joey
cow...calf	lion...cub
chicken...chick	monkey...baby
deer...fawn	pig...piglet, shoat
dog...pup	rabbit...bunny
duck...duckling	seal...pup
elephant...calf	sheep...lamb
fish...fry	swan...cygnet
frog...tadpole	tiger...cub
goat...kid	whale...calf
goose...gosling	zebra...colt

5. **Animal Nursery Rhymes**. If there are any young children visiting with pets, you can ask the participants to say some nursery rhymes about animals with the children, such as "Baa baa black sheep," "Mary had a little lamb," "Three little kittens," "Hey diddle diddle." As an alternative, you could ask one of the participants to read or to recite a poem to the children about animals, such as "The Owl and the Pussycat" or "The Calico Cat and the Gingham Dog."

Down Memory Lane

6. **Notable Pets.** Give the names of the following animals and see if the participants remember with whom or what they were associated:

> Sandy, the dog - **Little Orphan Annie**
> Fala, the dog - **Franklin Roosevelt**
> Baby, the leopard - **the movie "Bringing Up Baby"**
> Toto, the dog - **Dorothy's dog in "The Wizard of Oz"**
> Morris, the cat - **television commercials**
> King, the husky - **"Sergeant Preston," radio and TV shows**
> Rin Tin Tin, the dog - **movie star**
> Lassie, the dog - **early television star**
> Tigger, the tiger - **character in Winnie the Pooh stories**
> Checkers, the dog - **Richard Nixon's, when vice-president**
> Felix, the cat - **comic strip**
> The Cheshire Cat - *Alice in Wonderland*

7. **"Cats."** Tell the participants about the musical "Cats." You could read them one of the poems on which it is based (T.S. Eliot's *Old Possum's Book of Practical Cats*), play excerpts from the soundtrack, and/or show pictures of the actors in their costumes (from the record album or the piano music album).

DISCUSSION

1. Did any of you ever have any pets that were unusual—turtles, monkeys, snakes, etc. Tell us about your pet. How was it different from having a dog or a cat?

2. Did any of you live on a farm? What kinds of animals did you have? Did you help with their care? Did all of the animals help with the working of the farm? How?

3. Have all of you been to zoos? Can any of you tell us about any zoos or zoo animals that you particularly remember?

4. Have any of you been to Africa or India and seen animals in the wild? Can you share your memory of it with us?

> You could close the session by serving animal crackers.

PHOTOGRAPHS

IN THE MOOD

Music Possibilities - A piano playing popular songs of 1890-1930 or Scott Joplin's ragtime music.

Visual Possibilities

1. All the old black-and-white photographs you can beg or borrow. Everyone on the staff over 30 should have some black-and-white pictures, but the older the pictures the better.

2. Large picture of an old camera on display, especially one on a tripod with the cloth cover and powder flash. Stereoscope or a picture of one. (You might be able to borrow one of these from an antique shop. You can find pictures in an early Sears catalog, such as 1902.)

3. Photographs of famous Americans, especially if you can find pictures of them with their families.

ACTIVITIES

1. **Old Photographs**. Ask the participants to bring any old photos they have that are important to them. Ask everyone to share their pictures and what they mean to them. With a large group, you might ask each participant to bring only 2-3 pictures. Also, share a picture of your family or yourself when a child.

2. **Baby Pictures**. Ask participants to bring baby pictures of themselves (or as young a picture as they have) to share with the others. You could gather them in advance, put them on a poster board, and let the other participants guess who is who.

3. **Home Movies**. A staff member might share a few minutes of some old eight mm home movies of their family. Staff might also be willing to bring in baby pictures and participants can guess who is who.

4. **Old Cameras**. You might be able to borrow or rent an old camera, like a Brownie, to show the participants. If it still works, buy film and take pictures of everyone. Check these places for cameras: antique shops, camera stores (some sell used camera equipment), staff or family members, pawn shops. There might be a local collector who would be willing to show off his or her old cameras.

5. **Photograph Studios**. There are photo studios throughout the country that specialize in taking pictures that look as if they were taken decades ago, with old clothes and scenery as props. Contact one of these studios to ask if the owner or manager would be willing to give a demonstration or to talk about how they create these pictures.

6. **Artistic Photographs**. Invite a local amateur photographer to show some of his or her favorite artistic photos. This would be of particular interest to your group if the pictures were of local places.

7. **Developing**. Ask a local photographer to explain how pictures are made, developed, and printed—bringing in some of the equipment to show. It would be even more interesting if information was given about how photography has evolved over the last century.

8. **Taking Pictures**. If you have an instant camera and not too large a group, take a picture to give to each participant. *Or*, take a picture of each person with a noninstant camera and give to them after they are developed and printed. *Or*, set a camera on a tripod and take a picture of the whole group, including yourself. Later, after it's developed, make an enlargement for display. (Picture-taking would be a good closing activity for the session.)

DISCUSSION

1. Do any of you remember the first time you had a picture taken of yourself? How old were you? Do you remember who was taking the picture? Do you remember anything about the camera?

2. Do any of you remember the first time you used a camera? Do you remember the first camera you owned? What did you have to do to make it take pictures?

3. Where did you go to have the pictures developed and printed? Did any of you ever do your own darkroom work?

4. Have any of you ever gone to a studio to have formal pictures taken? What was the occasion?

5. Have any of you ever had home movies taken of you? Were you surprised at how you looked?

6. Did any of you have a stereoscope in your home? Tell us about it.

The sharing of pictures should bring out a great deal of discussion, too.

ROARING TWENTIES

IN THE MOOD

Music Possibilities

1. Play popular songs of the 1920s. (See Appendix B.) The following songs particularly capture the flavor of that decade:

"Five Foot Two, Eyes of Blue"	"Charleston"
"Ain't We Got Fun"	"Ten Cents a Dance"
"Ain't She Sweet"	"Varsity Drag"
"Ma! He's Making Eyes At Me"	"Makin' Whoopee"
"Yes Sir, That's My Baby"	"If You Knew Susie"

2. Presta Sounds has a tape, "Dance Party a la 1920s." Also, there are other recordings of original 1920s music available. Check your library. Also, look for early recordings by Paul Whiteman, Louis Armstrong, Duke Ellington.

Visual Possibilities

1. Pictures of personalities famous in the 1920s. See list under Activity #4. (Dover Publications has a good book called *Muray's Celebrity Portraits of the Twenties and Thirties*.)

2. Pictures of objects reminiscent of the 1920s: peekaboo hat, hip flask, a flapper (straight, short, fringed dress with many beads), old radio (especially a crystal set), a Ford Model T, Lindbergh's plane ("The Spirit of St. Louis"), ukelele, cigarette holder, long necklace of beads, raccoon coat.

Down Memory Lane

ACTIVITIES

1. **Dancing**. (Covered in more detail in the chapter "Dancing.")

    A. Ask a staff member to demonstrate the Charleston. (A good way to start or end the session.)

    B. Invite a local dance teacher and partner to demonstrate several dances of the 1920s, such as the Charleston, fox trot, black bottom, shimmy.

    C. Ask the participants to share their memories about the following aspects of dancing in the 1920s: tea dances; button shining (dancing with bodies pressed close together); "Ten cents a dance" halls (young women, called "taxi drivers," were paid ten cents for each dance with a customer); dance marathons.

2. **Fads**. Ask the participants if they remember any of the following fads:

    crossword puzzles
    mah-jongg
    flagpole sitting (the most famous sitter was "Shipwreck Kelly")
    barnstorming and flying stunts
    contract bridge
    rocking chair derbies
    "The Bunion Derby" (a cross-country foot race)

3. **1920s Slang**.

    bee's knees, berries, cat's meow, cat's whiskers, cat's pajamas - **wonderful**
    cake-eater, lounge lizard, jazzbo, jellybean - **ladies' man**
    nifty, hotsy-totsy - **something liked**
    sheik - **a sexy man**
    sheba - **a sexy woman**
    carry a torch - **unrequited love**
    hard-boiled egg - **tough guy**
    go fly a kite - **go away**
    Bronx cheer, raspberry - **a loud noise of disapproval**
    gam - **a girl's leg**
    hooch, booze, giggle water, giggle soup - **bootleg liquor**
    speakeasy, gin mill, whoopee parlor - **a bar that sold illegal liquor**
    hot diggity dog - **that's great!**
    goofy - **funny, strange**
    and how, I should hope to tell you - **agreeing with someone**
    for crying out loud - **said when exasperated**
    copacetic - **good, excellent, wonderful**
    scram - **get out of here!**
    buggy, jalopy - **car**
    hokum, applesauce, horsefeathers, banana oil, baloney - **nonsense**
    neck, pet - **kissing and hugging**

4. **People**. Ask the participants to identify (with pictures, if possible) and tell what they remember about the following personalities:

    Robert Benchley - **humorist**
    Edna St. Vincent Millay - **poet**
    H.L. Mencken - **reporter, critic, writer**
    Eugene O'Neill - **dramatist** ("Beyond the Horizon," "Emperor Jones")
    Sinclair Lewis - **author** (*Main Street* and *Babbitt*)
    Billy Sunday - **evangelist, baseball player**
    Bernard Baruch - **financier**
    Aimee Semple McPherson - **evangelist**
    Eddie Rickenbacker - **pilot, World War I ace**
    William Jennings Bryan - **lawyer, Scopes trial prosecuter, presidential contender**
    Clarence Darrow - **defense lawyer** (Scopes trial)
    Richard Byrd - **Antarctic explorer**
    Marcus Garvey - **Jamaican organizer of back-to-Africa movement**
    Will Rogers - **humorist, political satirist**
    Alfred Smith - **New York governor, ran for president in 1928**
    Jimmy Walker - **New York City mayor**
    Dorothy Parker - **humorist**
    Heywood Broun - **columnist**
    Irving Berlin - **songwriter**
    Babe Ruth - **baseball player and home run champ**
    Duke Ellington - **jazz composer, pianist, and bandleader**
    Louis Armstrong - **trumpeter, bandleader**
    Paul Whiteman - **bandleader, commissioned "Rhapsody in Blue"**

5. **Music**. Sing some of the better-known popular songs of the 1920s. Ask if any of these were particular favorites of anyone. Examples:

    "Five Foot Two, Eyes of Blue"   "Ain't She Sweet"
    "Toot Toot Tootsie"   "Yes Sir, That's My Baby"
    "I'm Forever Blowing Bubbles"   "Carolina in the Morning"
    "Ma, He's Making Eyes at Me"   "Sweetheart of Sigma Chi"
    "Button Up Your Overcoat"   "Baby Face"
    "Bye Bye Blackbird"   "Side by Side"

6. **News Stories**. Ask the participants what they remember about the following news stories:

    Lindbergh's flight across the Atlantic, 1927
    Tour of the U.S. by Edward, Prince of Wales, 1924
    Scopes "Monkey" Trial, 1925
    Death of Rudolph Valentino, 1926
    Teapot Dome Scandal, early 1920s
    Death of President Harding, 1923
    St. Valentine's Day Massacre, 1929

7. **Styles.** Ask the participants if they remember the fashions that were popular in the 1920s. Ask them to describe the following 1920s styles and if they ever wore them. (If you have any of the clothes, wear them!)

        patent-leather hair   cloche hats
        galoshes   bobbed hair
        golf hose   knickers
        slicker   oxford bags (men's pants)
        peekaboo hat   raccoon coat
        saddle shoes   zoot suit
        flapper dress   argyle socks
        turned-down hose

8. **Related Activity.** Edna St. Vincent Millay wrote poems that captured the spirit of the decade. If you have a reading group, read some of her poems.

DISCUSSION

1. Were any of you flappers or sheiks during the 1920s? How did you dress? Where did you go to have fun? What is the wildest thing you did? Did any of you play the ukelele or wear a raccoon coat? When did you stop being a sheik or a flapper?

2. Can any of you remember when you first got your hair bobbed? What was your family's reaction?

3. How did you feel about Prohibition? Did any of you work to enforce it? Did any of you ever make your own liquor? How many of you ever went to a speakeasy? What were they like?

4. What kind of car did you drive? Did you ever ride in a rumble seat?

5. How did you react to the news that the stock market was in trouble in October of 1929?

6. Can some of you share what was the most important event that happened to you, personally, during the 1920s?

ROOSEVELT and the THIRTIES

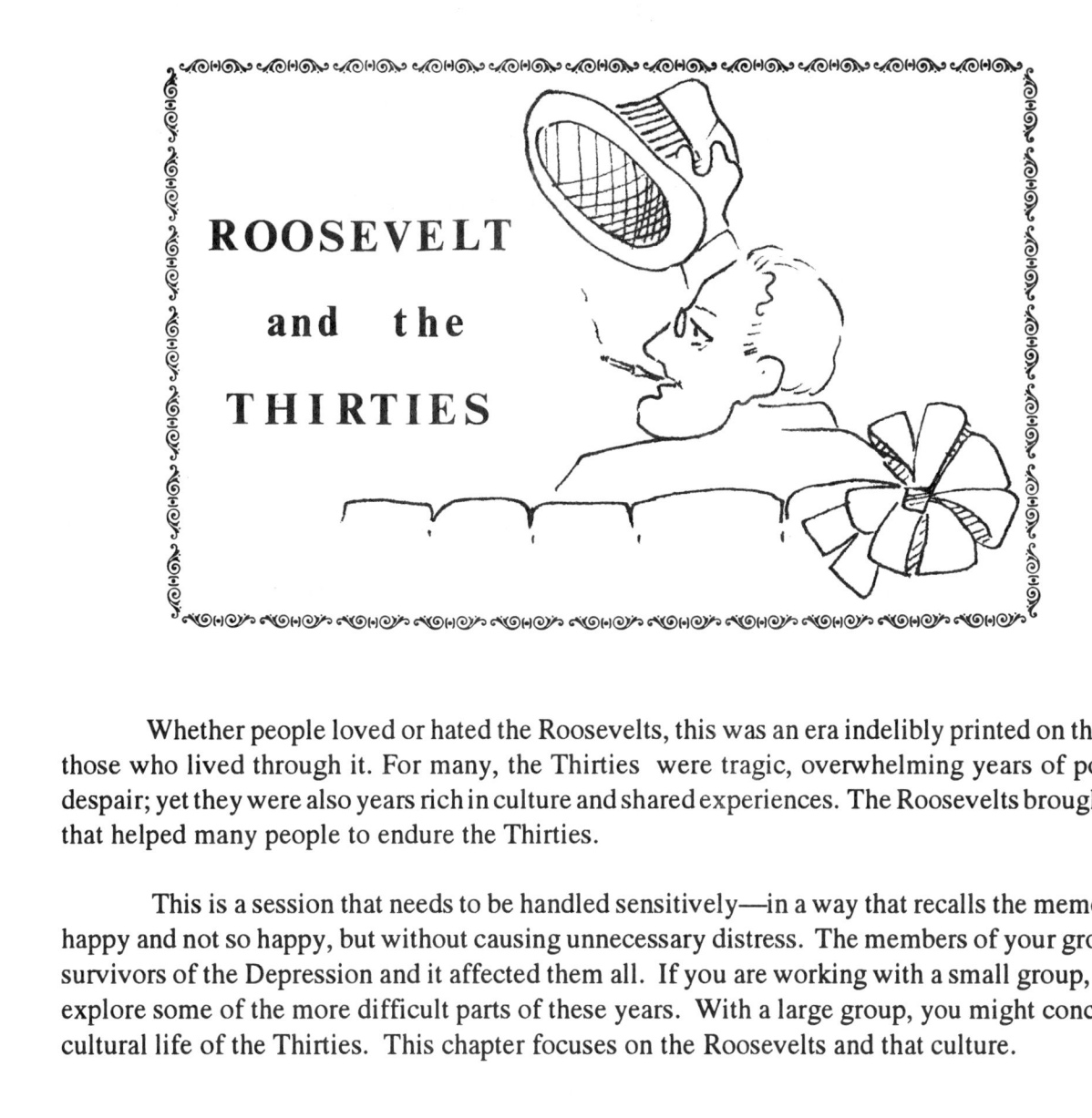

Whether people loved or hated the Roosevelts, this was an era indelibly printed on the minds of those who lived through it. For many, the Thirties were tragic, overwhelming years of poverty and despair; yet they were also years rich in culture and shared experiences. The Roosevelts brought the hope that helped many people to endure the Thirties.

This is a session that needs to be handled sensitively—in a way that recalls the memories, both happy and not so happy, but without causing unnecessary distress. The members of your group are the survivors of the Depression and it affected them all. If you are working with a small group, you could explore some of the more difficult parts of these years. With a large group, you might concentrate on cultural life of the Thirties. This chapter focuses on the Roosevelts and that culture.

IN THE MOOD

Music Possibilities

1. Popular songs of the 1930s. (See Appendix B.) These songs are particularly associated with the 1930s:

    "In a Shanty In Old Shanty Town"
    "Tumbling Tumbleweeds"
    "Brother, Can You Spare a Dime"
    "Happy Days Are Here Again"
    "We're In the Money" ("The Gold-diggers' Song")
    "Life Is Just a Bowl Of Cherries"

2. Presta Sounds has a tape entitled "Songs of the Depression." (See Appendix A.)

3. Big band music of the 1930s (Glenn Miller, Duke Ellington, Guy Lombardo, Benny Goodman, etc.).

Visual Possibilities

1. Pictures of Franklin and Eleanor Roosevelt and the White House.

2. Pictures of well-known personalities of the 1930s. See list under Activity #1.

3. Old *Look* or *Life* magazines from the 1930s.

4. Sheet music of songs popular in the 1930s. (See Appendix B.)

ACTIVITIES

1. **People**. Name some of the following personalities from the Thirties and have the participants identify them. If you can find pictures of any of these people or others from that era, see if the participants can recognize any of them. (See Dover Publications' *Muray's Celebrity Portraits of the Twenties and Thirties*.)

Kate Smith - **singer, radio personality**
Major Bowes - **host of radio's "Original Amateur Hour"**
Orson Welles - **actor, filmmaker**
Shirley Temple - **child actress**
Harry Hopkins - **headed FDR's federal relief program**
Babe Didrickson Zaharias - **Olympic athlete, pro golfer**
Pepper Martin - **baseball player**
Bobby Jones - **golf pro**
Jack Armstrong - **radio's "All American Boy"**
Tom Mix - **made cowboy movies**
John Dillinger - **notorious bank thief**
Bonnie Parker and Clyde Barrow - **bank robbing team**
Will Rogers - **humorist and political satirist**
Frances Perkins - **FDR's labor secretary and the first woman cabinet officer**
Brenda Frazier - **debutante, "Glamor Girl"**
Elsa Maxwell - **lavish hostess**
Cole Porter - **composer of popular songs**
Barbara Hutton - **Woolworth heiress**
John L. Lewis - **labor leader**
Marie Dressler - **movie star**
Louella Parsons - **gossip columnist**
William Powell - **actor, played "The Thin Man"**
Huey Long - **Louisiana senator and governor**
Westbrook Pegler - **columnist who was anti-Roosevelt**
Harry James - **trumpeter and bandleader**
Alf Landon - **Republican who ran against FDR in 1936**
Father Charles E. Coughlin - **radio preacher**
Artie Shaw - **clarinetist and bandleader**
Helen O'Connell - **female vocalist with the big bands**

Billie Holiday - **blues singer**
The Andrews Sisters - **singing trio**
Mary McLeod Bethune - **African-American educator**
Pearl Buck - **author, won the Nobel prize for literature in 1938 for** *The Good Earth*
Clarence Darrow - **defense lawyer**
W.E.B. DuBois - **African-American educator and writer**
Amelia Earhart - **aviator, first woman to fly the Atlantic**
Marcus Garvey - **Jamaican leader**
Ernest Hemingway - **journalist and novelist**
Oliver Wendell Holmes - **U.S. Supreme Court Justice**
Margaret Sanger - **nurse and birth control pioneer**
Frank Lloyd Wright - **architect**
Richard Byrd - **Polar explorer**
George Washington Carver - **botanist**

2. **Music**. If you have sheet music for songs of the 1930s and someone to play them, sing these songs with the participants. If you have recordings, play them for listening and singing. Ask the participants if they have any memories associated with the songs: where they first heard the song, who made them famous, if the songs have any special meanings for anyone. (See Appendix B for specific song suggestions.) The following songs are some that have historical importance:

"Happy Days are Here Again" - Roosevelt's theme song
"Brother, Can you Spare a Dime?" - about the Depression
"Who's Afraid of the Big, Bad Wolf?" - a popular song because people thought of the Depression as the big, bad wolf
"Tumbling Tumbleweeds" - about the dry desertland of the Southwest after the Dust Bowl
"September Song" - Kurt Weill's comment about the situation in Europe in 1938
"God Bless America" - Irving Berlin's pre-World War II patriotic song
"My Lord, What a Mourning" - was played on the radio on the day Roosevelt died

3. **New Deal Programs**. Ask the participants if they can remember what these initials stood for, what these programs did, and/or how they may have benefitted from them.

NRA - National Recovery Act or Administration; regulated wages and working hours. Slogan, "We do our part." The symbol was the Blue Eagle. Parades and rallies were held to promote it.

WPA - Works Progress Administration; hired artists, designers, builders, and craftsmen and gave them projects.

FERA - Federal Emergency Relief Administration; gave money to states for welfare.

CCC - Civilian Conservation Corps; for unemployed men, 18-25, who worked on conservation and reforestation projects.

PWA - Public Works Administration; financed the building of bridges, dams, tunnels, etc.

TVA - Tennessee Valley Authority; developed the Tennessee River Valley.

HOLC - Home Owners' Loan Corporation; gave new loans to homeowners who were in danger of losing their homes.

AAA - Agricultural Adjustment Act; crop curtailment and refinancing of farm mortgages.

NYA - National Youth Administration; student aid to youth 16-25.

4. **Popular Culture of the 1930s**. Name these things from the popular culture and ask the participants what they remember about them:

Ballyhoo magazine - humorous and satirical, it spoofed the culture
Esquire - The "Magazine for Men," it used articles by big name authors
"Snow White and the Seven Dwarfs" - first feature-length cartoon
The Big Apple - popular dance of 1937; "Do that stomp with lots of pomp."
"Gone With the Wind" - popular novel of the 1930s about life in the South around the Civil War
"Knock, knock" jokes - a craze in the 1930s
"The March of Time" newsreels - news shorts shown in the movie theaters
Depression glass and Fiesta ware - dishes commonly sold in the 1930s; at the movies there was "Depression Giveaway Dish Night"
Cafe Society - the social world of the wealthy youth
Art Deco - a style of decorating
Washington Merry-Go-Round - popular book by Drew Pearson and Robert Allen
Gangster movies - "Little Caesar," "Public Enemy," "Scarface," with stars such as Jimmy Cagney, Edward G. Robinson, Humphrey Bogart
Fred Astaire and Ginger Rogers - movie dance team
Mae West - actress and movie star of risque films
"Porgy and Bess" - George Gershwin's opera in the jazz idiom
Riding the rails - travelling the country by hitching a ride on a freight train

5. **Headlines of the 1930s**. Ask the participants to recall the following news events: You could ask, "What do you remember about. . ."

Repeal of Prohibition, 1933
The Great Bank Holiday, March 1933
Kidnapping of the Lindbergh baby, March 1932
Birth of the Dionne quintuplets, 1934
Election of Franklin Roosevelt, November 1932
Burning of the cruise liner "Morro Castle," 1934
Assassination of Huey Long, 1935
Abdication of King Edward VIII to marry Wallis Simpson, 1936
Dust Bowl, 1932
Olympics in Los Angeles, 1932
Olympics in Berlin—Jesse Owen was the star, 1936
Disappearance of Amelia Earhart, 1937
Marion Anderson singing at the Washington Monument, 1939
Explosion of the dirigible "Hindenburg," 1937
Coronation of George VI in England, 1937
New York World's Fair of 1939-40

Depending on your group, you also might want to ask how the Depression affected each of them and what they did to survive it.

6. **Related Activity.** The book *Growing Up* by Russell Baker gives a realistic, yet totally enjoyable, picture of growing up in the Depression. This book could be read aloud to the participants.

7. **Related Activity.** See the movie "You Can't Take It With You," based on a humorous play about a family in the Depression.

DISCUSSION

1. Can some of you share your happiest, or most vivid, memory of the 1930s?

2. People had very strong feelings about Franklin Roosevelt. Can some of you share what you remember the most about him and how you felt about him at the time?

3. Did any of you own a Scottie like the Roosevelt's dog Fala? What was your dog's name?

4. How much were any of you aware of FDR's polio and disability while he was president?

5. How many of you listened to FDR's Fireside Chats? Can any of you remember some of the things he talked about? Were any of you present at the Inauguration? How many of you listened to it on the radio? How did his Inaugural address make you feel?

6. Mrs. Roosevelt travelled a great deal. Did any of you ever see her or talk to her? Can anyone remember the kinds of things she wrote in her column "My Day"? Can some of you share any memories of her and what she did as the president's wife?

7. Can any of you remember what you were doing when you heard that Franklin Roosevelt died? Did any of you see the funeral train or see any part of the funeral? How did most people react to his death?

SCHOOL DAYS

IN THE MOOD

Music Possibilities

1. Music written when the majority of the participants were in elementary school. Examples of well-known songs from early in this century:

"Bicycle Built for Two"	"East Side, West Side"
"After the Ball"	"My Country 'Tis of Thee"
"The Band Played On"	"In the Good Old Summertime"
"In My Merry Oldsmobile"	"I Love You Truly"
"Wait til the Sun Shines, Nellie"	"Meet Me in St. Louis"
"Take Me Out to the Ball Game"	"Oh, You Beautiful Doll"

2. Traditional children's songs that might have been sung in school. Examples:

"Baa, Baa Black Sheep"	"Mary had a Little Lamb"
"Skip To My Lou"	"Billy Boy"
"Comin' Through the Rye"	"Lazy Mary"
"Oh, Susanna"	"Polly Wolly Doodle"

3. College Songs. Examples: "Notre Dame Marching Song," "Whiffenpoof Song," "Boola Boola," "Sweetheart Of Sigma Chi," "On Wisconsin," "Fair Harvard."

4. Music referring to school and learning. Examples: "I've Got a Gal in Kalamazoo," "The ABCs," "'A'—You're Adorable," "School Days," "Do Re Mi," "This Old Man."

5. Foreign Language Songs, preferably of different languages.

Visual Possibilities

Display several school-related objects in the room. Suggestions: blackboard (can be used for keeping scores of any quizzes you might give *or* it can have a short phrase written on it 25 times), chalk, erasers, picture of schoolhouse, bottle of ink, school books (especially *McGuffey's Eclectic Readers*, which have been reprinted and are in bookstores and libraries), chart on the wall with the ABCs (upper and lower case), a large red apple, yardstick, maps (check old *National Geographic* magazines), pictures of presidents, school pennants, dunce cap and stool, lunch pails.

You can start the session by singing "School Days."

ACTIVITIES

The approach used in this session is a little different. The activities consist of having short quizzes on different school subjects. These can be done as teams or by just asking residents to call out the answers.

Arithmetic

1. Ask participants to do simple sums in their heads.

2. Ask questions about numbers. Examples:

> What number is unlucky? **13**
> How many zeroes are in one million? **6**
> Which inning is considered the lucky one in baseball? **7**
> What berth was considered lucky on the Pullman car? **Lower 7**
> How far is it to the sun? **93 million miles**
> How many American colonies were there? **13**
> What are snake eyes? **Two dice with one dot on each**
> What is a baker's dozen? **13**
> How many times are the banns of marriage called? **3**
> How many disciples of Jesus were there? **12**
> How many nights are there in Hanukah? **8**
> For how many nights did Scheherezade tell her stories? **1001**
> How many little Foys were there? **7**
> How long did it rain on Noah? **40 days and 40 nights**

Spelling - If you quiz individuals, pick words that that particular person will be able to spell.

1. Go around the group 2-3 times with progressively harder words from the dictionary. Four-syllable words are the hardest. Variation: Pick a word to spell for each letter of the alphabet.

2. Have participants spell words that were slang words during the 1920s. Examples:

copacetic	gam	flapper	jalopy	raspberry	sheba	sheik
speakeasy	high-hat	hooch	kisser	scram	spiffy	nerts
hokum	hoofer	hotsy-totsy	neck	ritzy	cake-eater	swanky

English/Reading

1. Use one of the "Madlibs" books, available in bookstores and card shops. Be prepared to refresh the participants' memories with examples of what some of the parts of speech are, such as adverbs and adjectives.

2. Give a word and have participants give an antonym. It can be simple or hard, depending on your group.

3. Ask participants to name homonyms. (Write them on the blackboard as they are named.) Example: to, too, two.

Geography

1. Ask participants to name state or national capitals. (Listed in any almanac or trivia encyclopedia.)

2. Ask participants to give locations of natural landmarks. (The chapter on Vacations has some appropriate questions. (See also *Memories, Dreams and Thoughts*.)

3. Have participants tell you their place of birth and mark it on a large map.

History

1. Have a short quiz on American history. (There are more questions in *Memories, Thoughts, and Dreams*. See Appendix A.)

> What first lady was a delegate to the First General Assembly of the United Nations?
> **Eleanor Roosevelt**
> For what occasion was the Gettysburg address delivered?
> **Dedication of the Gettysburg Cemetery**
> Who burned the city of Washington in 1812?
> **The British**
> What territory did Jefferson purchase that doubled the size of the United States?
> **Louisiana territory, from France**
> The "S" in Harry S. Truman is an initial for what?
> **Nothing**
> Which president was in office the longest?
> **Franklin Roosevelt**
> Who was the oldest president to be inaugurated?
> **Ronald Reagan**
> Who was the heaviest president?
> **William Howard Taft—322 pounds**
> Who was the first female cabinet member?
> **Frances Perkins**

2. If you can find reproductions of pictures of famous historical events, ask participants if they can identify the event. (Check your local library, art museum, or history text.)

Foreign Languages

1. Ask the meanings of foreign phrases. Examples:

"C'est la vie."	**That's life.**
"a la mode"	**with ice cream** (literally, "in the style")
"ad infinitum"	**forever**
"et cetera"	**and so on**
"aloha"	**hello, good-bye**
"arrivederci"	**until we meet again**
"Que sera sera"	**Whatever will be will be**
"Je ne sais quoi"	**a thing hard to describe or express**
"PDQ"	**right away** ("pretty damn quick")
"Sic semper tyrannis"	**Thus ever to tyrants**
"shalom"	**hello, good-bye, peace**
"e pluribus unum"	**out of many, one** (U. S. motto)

2. Play short passages of people talking or singing in foreign languages and ask participants to identify the language. Use common ones, like German, French, Irish, Scottish, Spanish, Russian, Yiddish. If you have several participants of one ethnic group, use that language. If you have an ethnically-mixed staff, record them!

Related Activity. Ask a local elementary school teacher to come and talk about schools today. A teacher who just retired or who is near retirement could give a perspective on the change in schools. Some of your group might like to take a trip to a local school.

DISCUSSION

If you live in a small town and many of your participants grew up there, take pictures of your local schools to enhance the discussion. Your local historical society might have old pictures of the schools.

1. Did any of you go to a one-room schoolhouse? How did the teacher organize the class so that everyone could learn? How many were in the school?

2. Were any of you teachers? Have any of you taught in a one-room schoolhouse? Was it easier or harder than teaching just one class? What subjects did you teach? What kind of diploma did you need in order to be hired? If you didn't go to a one-room schoolhouse, what was your school like?

3. Can some of you share how you got to school? (A slang phrase for walking was "shank's mare.") Were there schoolbells to tell you when school started? Did you carry a lunch pail or go home for lunch? Was your schoolhouse red? (Red was usually the cheapest paint available.)

4. Do any of you remember the names of any of your school books? Did the school provide them or did you have to buy them? With what materials did you learn to write?

5. Can any of you remember having a favorite teacher or one who particularly inspired you? Tell us about this person.

6. Do any of you remember your first day of school? Tell us about it.

7. Can some of you share how you were disciplined in school?

8. Have any of you ever gone to a school class reunion? Was it a pleasant or unpleasant experience? Have any of you kept in contact with any of your school friends? Did any of you marry your high school sweetheart?

9. Did any of you ever give an apple to your teacher? Do you remember giving any other gifts?

At the end of the session, sing "School Days" again and serve apple slices.

SHOPPING

IN THE MOOD

Music Possibilities

1. Appropriate songs:

    "I Found a Million Dollar Baby (in a 5 and 10 Cent Store)"
    "The Wells Fargo Wagon" (from the musical "The Music Man")
    "Who Will Buy" (from the musical "Oliver")
    "That Great Come-and-Get-It Day" (from the musical "Finian's Rainbow")
    "Love for Sale" (by Cole Porter)
    "Molly Malone" (traditional folk song)

2. Play any music from 1915-1945 (original recordings, if possible).

Visual Possibilities

1. Old and new Sears and Montgomery Ward catalogs.

2. Pictures of early stores. Or, if you have any stores in your area that capture the essence of a store from the 1920s or 1930s (like the candy counter at Farrell's ice cream shops), take pictures and make enlargements to show.

3. Set up a display table in your activity room that would have examples of what you could have bought in an old general store. Examples: peppermint sticks, gumdrops, Babe Ruth bars, Mail Pouch tobacco, pickles, dry beans, fruit, cured meats, cheese chunks (under a glass cover), thread, notions, yard goods. The following products were used decades ago and are still available: Morton Salt, Old Dutch Cleanser, Maxwell House Coffee, Coca-Cola, Ivory Soap, Gold Medal Flour.

ACTIVITIES

1. **Store Items**. Show the items you gathered for your display table. Ask the participants if they remember any specific brand names for the items.

2. **Store Items**. Ask the participants to name items that could be bought in a general store or by mail-order catalog in the 1920s and 1930s. You could ask them to name items for each letter in the alphabet. Or ask the participants what items could be bought in specialty stores, such as drug stores, hardware stores, etc. Ask what other kinds of stores they may have frequented and what products were sold. If you live in a small town, take pictures of the older, established stores and ask the participants what they remember about them.

3. **Catalogs**. Give each participant a copy of a page from an old catalog, particularly of objects no longer common or available. Ask each one to tell the others what is on the page and the prices. For an interesting comparison, pick items that are found in both an old and a new catalog and put copies of these pages side by side. (If you don't have any old reprinted catalogs, see *Good Old Days* magazines.)

4. **Prices**. If you have both old and new Sears or Ward catalogs, make a list of old and new prices on common items. Give the old price and ask the participants to guess what the current price is, or vice versa. Item suggestions: large appliances (stoves, washing machines, ice boxes/refrigerators), bicycles, jewelry, clothes, writing materials, pots and pans, cameras, kitchen gadgets, silverware, crystal, musical instruments, hardware, blankets. (The book *Memories, Dreams and Thoughts* has a list of the cost of items from the early 1900s.)

5. **Catalog Items**. Name these catalog items and ask the participants to describe what they are:

    spectacles - **eyeglasses, wire-rimmed**
    hearing horn - **a long, bell-shaped tube to enhance hearing**
    stereoscope - **an optical instrument with two lenses; a person looked at two pictures of the same scene, but one picture appeared with a three-dimensional look**
    gramophone - **an early phonograph, it had a bell-shaped speaker**
    chamois - **an animal skin used for cleaning wood or glass**
    wringer - **it squeezed the water out of clothes after washing**
    cuspidor - **a receptacle for men's spit when indoors**
    Murphy bed - **a bed that folded up against the wall when not in use**
    chiffonier - **a high, narrow chest of drawers**
    wardrobe - **a free-standing, moveable wooden closet**
    divan - **sofa**

6. **Products**. Name these household and medicinal products and have the participants describe their use:

    Mrs. Winslow's Soothing Syrup - **for toothache, it was rubbed on the gums**
    Lydia Pinkham's Vegetable Compound - **for "female trouble"**
    Carter's Little Nerve Pills - **for nervousness and indigestion**
    Dr. Sloan's Liniment - **for sore muscles and joints, external use**
    castor oil - **a very thorough laxative**
    tincture of arnica - **bruises and swellings**

camphorated oil - **external treatment for coughs and sore throats**
glycerine - **external use; softener, moistener, or lubricant**
petroleum jelly - **external use; bruises, cuts, burns, chaps**
carbolic acid - **disinfectant**
witch hazel - **external use; wounds, sprains, stiff joints**
depilatory - **chemical for removing hair**
olive wax pomatum - **for waxing hair down**
calomel - **purgative and fungicide**
paregoric - **lessens pain**

DISCUSSION

1. Can any of you remember the names of the department stores where you most frequently shopped? Did you prefer the local department stores or the chain stores? Do you remember the names of other stores you used when you were younger? (drug, hardware, dime store, shoes, grocery, clothing, candy)

2. What is cash and carry? Do any of you remember the first time you bought on credit? When was that? How did you feel about it?

3. Do any of you remember helping your mother shop? What was the store you used most often? What were the stores like before the coming of supermarkets and big discount stores?

4. Did any of you order from Sears or Ward catalogs? Did you do it occasionally or did you buy most of what you needed from catalogs? Did the merchandise measure up to what was written in the catalog? When you ordered something, how did the merchandise arrive?

At the close of the session, give the participants something to eat from your display table, e.g., a slice of cheese, peppermint stick, pickle, or gumdrops.

SPORTS

IN THE MOOD

Music Possibilities

1. Sports-related songs:

   "Take Me Out To the Ballgame" "Notre Dame Victory Song"
   "You Gotta be a Football Hero" "Heart" (from "Damn Yankees")
   "The Star Spangled Banner" (sung before games)

2. Soundtrack to "Damn Yankees."

3. College alumni songs.

4. Recording of Abbott and Costello's famous "Who's on First" routine.

5. Presta Sounds has a tape recording of Bill Stern's "Sports Newsreel."

Visual Possibilities

1. Display table: sports equipment—bat, balls (all types), mitts, shoulder pads, tennis rackets, baseball hats or football helmets, golf clubs, badminton rackets and birdie, etc.

2. Pictures of sports heroes of the past or pictures of people playing sports.

3. College banners.

4. Olympic symbol.

Down Memory Lane

ACTIVITIES

1. **Equipment.** Show all the sports equipment you have gathered. Hold up an object and ask the participants what it is and in what sport it is used. Ask if any of them ever played that sport. Try to find some equipment for some less well-known sports, too, such as rugby, racketball, or cricket. (Ask staff or families to bring in some objects.)

2. **Heroes.** Ask the participants to name their favorite sports stars of the past. If you have found pictures of some well-known sports heroes, show them and ask if anyone can identify the people. Name the heroes on the following list and have the participants name the sport. You could also ask them to share any memories they might have about that person. For those with nicknames, give that name first and see if the participants can give their real name.

    "Sultan of Swat" or "Bambino" - **Babe Ruth, baseball**
    "The Norwegian Doll" - **Sonya Henie, figure skating**
    "Yankee Clipper" or "Joltin' Joe" - **Joe DiMaggio, baseball**
    "The Brown Bomber" - **Joe Louis, boxing**
    "The Manassa Mauler" - **Jack Dempsey, boxing**
    "The Galloping Ghost of Illinois" - **Red Grange, football**
    "Miss Poker Face" - **Helen Wills Moody, tennis**
    "Slammin' Sammy" - **Sam Snead, golf**
    "The Georgia Peach" or "Tyrus the Greatest" - **Ty Cobb, baseball**
    "The Brockton Blockbuster" - **Rocky Marciano, boxing**
    "Wild Bull of Pampas" - **Luis Angel Firpo, boxing**
    "Tempestuous Ted" - **Ted Williams, baseball**
    "Larrupin' Lou" or "The Iron Horse" - **Lou Gehrig, baseball**
    "World's Fastest Human" - **Charley Paddock, track**
    "Big Bill" Tilden - **tennis**
    Esther Williams - **Olympic diving, synchronized swimming**
    Jim Thorpe - **Olympic track, football**
    Gertrude Ederle - **swimming, first American to swim the English channel in 1926**
    Babe Didrickson Zaharias - **Olympic track, golf**
    Johnny Weismuller - **Olympic swimming**
    Bobby Jones - **golf**
    Max Schmeling - **boxing**
    Jesse Owen - **Olympic track and field**
    Satchel Paige - **baseball (pitcher)**
    Jackie Robinson - **first black major league baseball player**
    Knute Rockne - **Notre Dame football coach**
    Red Barber - **baseball announcer**
    Judge Kenesaw Mountain Landis - **baseball's first commissioner**
    Bill Klem - **baseball umpire for 40 years**
    Casey Stengel - **Yankee manager**

3. **Great Moments in Sports.** There are recordings available in libraries of great moments in sports history that you could play. Play excerpts, one at a time, and ask the participants to share their memories of the event.

4. **Sports**. Describe a sport and have the participants identify it. Ask if any have ever played each game. Examples:

    Competitors use clubs to hit small balls into holes in the ground. **golf**
    Two or four players hit small bouncing balls back and forth across a net. **tennis**
    Players hit a small hard ball with a stick and then run around a course. **baseball or cricket**
    A team of players tries to hit a large ball into a net without using their hands. **soccer**
    Players bounce a large ball across the floor and then try to throw it through a hoop. **basketball**
    Players move a small disk across ice and into a net. **ice hockey**
    Teams move a large, oblong ball from one side of a field to the other. **football**
    Players ride on horses and use sticks to hit a small ball across a field. **polo**
    A competitor uses a long pole to jump up and over a horizontal pole. **pole vaulting**
    Competitors try to be the first to cross a finish line. **track events**
    Competitors jump, do flips, vault, and swing on rings and bars. **gymnastics**
    Two opponents hit each other. **boxing**
    Competitors shoot arrows at a target. **archery**

5. **Speaker**. Invite a local retired sports writer or athlete to visit and to exchange memories with the participants about sports events and heroes of the past.

6. **Home Teams**. Name cities in the U.S. and ask what teams played there. Then ask each person to talk about his/her favorite team(s) of the past and the present.

    Brooklyn: Dodgers (baseball)
    New York: Giants (football); Yankees and Mets (baseball)
    Green Bay, Wisconsin: Packers (football)
    Baltimore: Colts (football); Orioles (baseball)
    Boston: Red Sox (baseball); Celtics (basketball)
    Chicago: White Sox and Cubs (baseball); Bears (football)
    Los Angeles: Dodgers (baseball); Lakers (basketball)
    Washington, D.C.: Senators (baseball); Redskins (football)
    St. Louis: Cardinals (baseball)
    Philadelphia: Phillies (baseball)
    Cincinnati: Reds (baseball)
    Pittsburgh: Steelers (football); Pirates (baseball)

7. **Related Activity**. If you have participants who are able and interested, take several to a local sporting event. Many groups have discount or free tickets available for special populations.

DISCUSSION

1. What kinds of sports did you play while growing up? Did any of you excel in any sport? Did any of you play sports in high school or college? In what sports did you participate as an adult?

2. Did any of you have a sports idol when you were growing up? Who was it? Did you ever see your hero in person? How did she or he inspire you?

3. Did any of you ever go to the Olympics? When and where was it? Tell us what you remember about it.

4. Do any of you remember listening to sporting events on the radio in the 1920s, 1930s, or 1940s? What events did you hear?

5. Did any of you attend big sporting events? Which ones? What do you remember about them?

6. What are your favorite sports today? What teams or players do you like?

   You could end the session by singing "Take Me Out to the Ballgame" and/or by passing around popcorn or crackerjacks. (Caution: Be aware of the possibility of choking.)

Good source: *Champions of American Sport*, The National Portrait Gallery, Smithsonian Institution, 1981, Harry N. Abrams, Inc., Publishers, New York.

SUPERSTITIONS

IN THE MOOD

Music Possibilities - Songs about magic and superstitions. Examples:

"It's Magic," recorded by Doris Day
"Born On a Friday," recorded by Cleo Laine
"Luck Be a Lady," from the musical "Guys and Dolls"
"Bali Ha'i," from the musical "South Pacific"
"Old Devil Moon," from the musical "Finian's Rainbow"
"That Ol' Black Magic"
"Bewitched," by Rodgers and Hart
"Love, Your Spell Is Everywhere"
"Spellbound"
"When You Wish Upon a Star"
"With a Little Bit Of Luck," from the musical "My Fair Lady"
"Three Coins In the Fountain"
"I'm Looking Over a Four-leaf Clover"

Visual Possibilities - Display several well-known superstitious objects. Examples:

Rabbit's foot - rubbing brings good luck
Ladder - walking under it brings bad luck
Black cat - bad luck if it crosses your path
Horseshoe over the door - good luck
Salt shaker - If it's spilled, throw a pinch of it over your left shoulder to prevent bad luck.
Apple - "An apple a day keeps the doctor away."
A large number 13 - bad luck
Four-leaf clover (or a picture) - finding one brings good luck

Picture of a rainbow and a pot of gold
Picture of a stork carrying a baby
Open umbrella - bad luck
Mirror - breaking it brings bad luck

This is a good session for Friday the 13th. You might begin this session by singing "I'm Looking Over a Four-leaf Clover."

ACTIVITIES

1. **Good Luck Charms**. In promoting this session, ask the participants to bring any good luck charms they have. In the session, ask them to tell the group about it.

2. **Superstitious Objects**. Using the objects you displayed in the room, ask the participants what superstition they know for each object, good and bad. (See Visual Possibilities.)

3. **Common Superstitions**. Say the beginning of a superstition and let the participants complete it. Then, ask the participants to name all the other supersitions they know. You might ask them if any of these have ever come true for any of them! In addition to the ones listed earlier, here are some of the more common ones:

>   If you step on a crack you. . .**break your mother's back**.
>
>   If you drop a coin in a wishing well. . .**you get your wish**.
>
>   You get your wish with a wishbone if you. . .**break off the bigger part**.
>
>   Touching frogs gives you. . .**warts**.
>
>   If you put a tooth under your pillow. . .**the tooth fairy exchanges it for a coin**.
>
>   If your ears ring. . .**someone is talking about you**.
>
>   Bad things come in. . .**threes**.
>
>   For good luck on the stage, someone must say to you. . .**"break a leg."**
>
>   If you kiss the blarney stone. . .**you'll have the gift of gab**.

4. **Fortune-telling**. With a small group, tell fortunes with tarot cards or a ouija board. Find a book of palm reading and "try your hand" at reading palms.

5. **Superstitions Today**. You might want to discuss some superstitions that are still used today and ask the participants if they use them or believe in them.

>   Saying "God bless you" when someone sneezes.
>
>   Knocking on wood for protection.
>
>   "Whenever someone goes into space (or to the moon), the weather is bad."
>
>   You can tell the sex of an unborn baby by the way the mother looks, by how much the baby moves, or by doing some simple tests.

6. **Just For Fun**. Here are some old, obscure superstitions to read to the participants:

    If you are bald, rub your head with goose dung and the hair will grow again.
    It is unlucky to meet a man with flat feet on Monday morning.
    To cure hiccups: Lick the index finger of your right hand and cross the front of your left shoe three times as you recite the Lord's prayer backwards.
    If you get a chill and are shivering, cure it by wrapping a spider in a raisin, then swallow it.
    To bring good luck, a baby should be rubbed with lard immediately after birth.

DISCUSSION

1. Were any of you born on the 13th of the month? Were any of you born on Friday the 13th? Has anyone had any memorable good luck or bad luck on the 13th of the month or on Friday the 13th?

2. When you were children, did you believe in Santa Claus? In the Easter bunny? In the tooth fairy?

3. For those of you who have children, can you remember being told any Old Wives' tales? Did anyone predict the sex of your child before it was born?

4. Did you ever have a good luck charm? Did you ever have a lucky article of clothing?

5. Have any of you ever performed in the theater? Do you remember any superstitions that were supposed to give the performance good or bad luck? (For example, saying "Break a leg" before performing or "Bad dress rehearsal, good opening night.")

6. Have any of you ever had your palm read or had your fortune told? Was any of it accurate? Have any of you ever used tarot cards or a ouija board?

7. When you were a bride, what did you wear that was old, new, borrowed, blue? Did any of you ever catch a bride's bouquet? If so, were you the next to be married? Did anyone throw rice or tie shoes to your car? Can any of you remember any other wedding customs or superstitions?

8. Do any of you know any cures for hiccups? Have any of you ever used any folk cures for illness, such as wearing a garlic bag around the neck to ward off colds?

9. Have any of you ever sent, or refused to send, a chain letter? What kind of luck did you have?

10. Do any of you remember any superstitions that your parents had? (especially from other cultures)

11. Can some of you share the secret to living a long life?

    You could end the session by giving everyone a good luck charm: a small horseshoe, a four-leaf clover (made from green construction paper), or a penny ("Find a penny, collect many.")

    For a more complete listing of superstitions, see *Memories, Dreams and Thoughts* or *The Fun Encyclopedia*. (See Appendix A.)

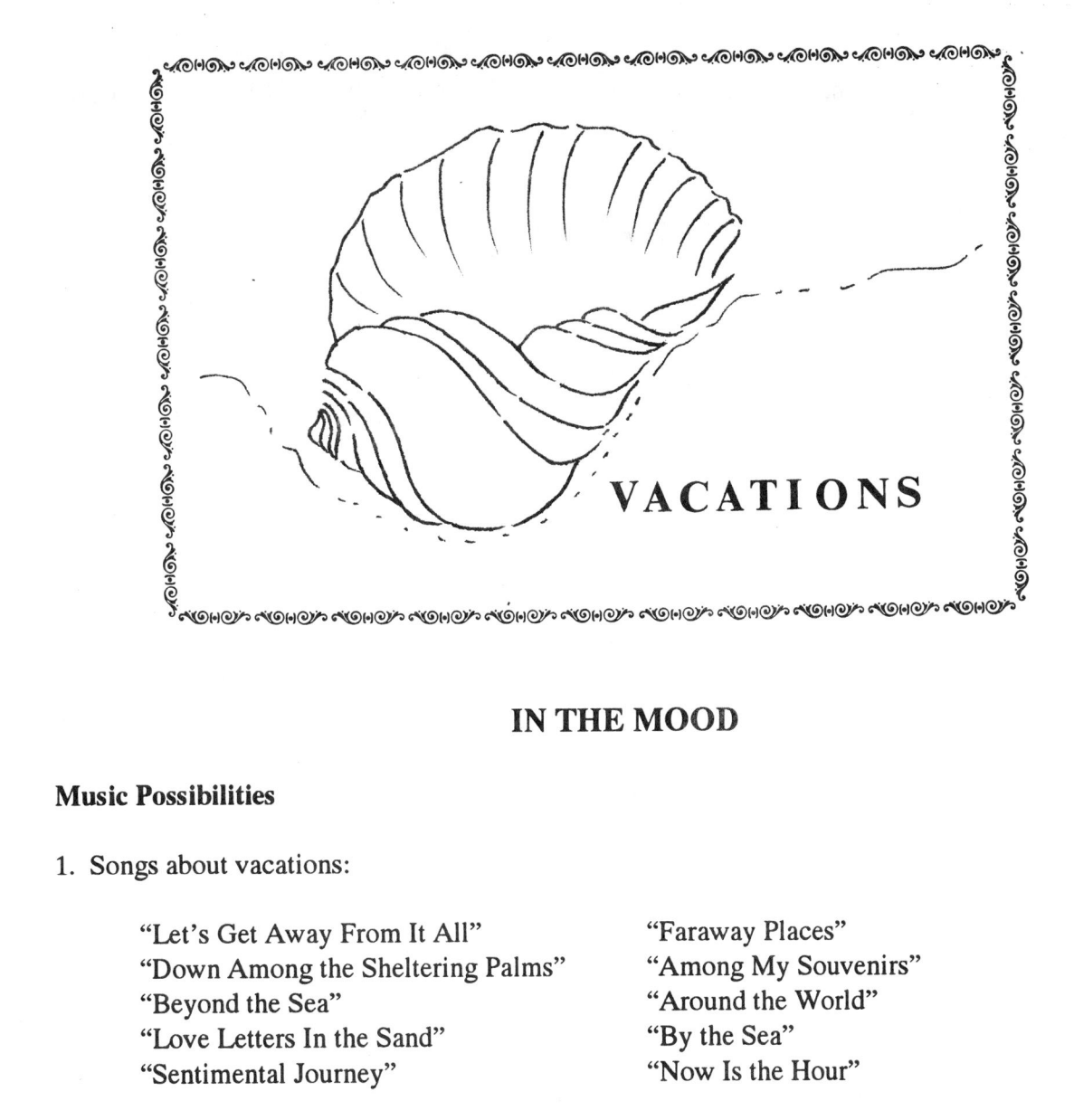

VACATIONS

IN THE MOOD

Music Possibilities

1. Songs about vacations:

   "Let's Get Away From It All"
   "Down Among the Sheltering Palms"
   "Beyond the Sea"
   "Love Letters In the Sand"
   "Sentimental Journey"

   "Faraway Places"
   "Among My Souvenirs"
   "Around the World"
   "By the Sea"
   "Now Is the Hour"

2. Songs about places:

   "Arrivederci, Roma"
   "A Foggy Day In London Town"
   "White Cliffs Of Dover"
   "Carolina In the Morning"
   "Down By the O-hi-o"
   "Moon Over Miami"
   "Alabamy Bound"
   "South Of the Border"
   "Beautiful Ohio"

   "Missouri Waltz"
   "I Love Paris"
   "Indiana"
   "California, Here I Come"
   "Blue Hawaii"
   "Old Cape Cod"
   "Bali Ha'i"
   "April In Paris"
   "How Ya Gonna Keep 'Em Down On the Farm"

Visual Possibilities

1. Travel posters. You can buy these from Paradise Products, M & N International, or Giant Photo. (See Appendix A.)

2. Display of items you would take on a vacation: swimsuits, sunglasses, walking sticks, fishing pole, suitcase, seashells, suntan lotion, knapsack, canteen, camera, foreign language dictionaries, currency conversion table.

ACTIVITIES

1. **To begin.** Ask: "If you could go anywhere in the world for a vacation, where would you like to go?"

2. **Music.** Sing songs together about faraway places. See list in Music Possibilities. Or, play "Name that Tune" with these same songs—play melodies and let the participants guess the place that is referred to in the song.

3. **American Vacation Spots.**

   Where is the fountain of youth?   **St. Augustine, Florida**
   In what state is historic Williamsburg?   **Virginia**
   Where is the Old North church where Paul Revere saw the lantern signals?   **Boston**
   In what state is Mt. Rushmore?   **South Dakota** (The presidents carved in stone there are Washington, Lincoln, Jefferson, and Theodore Roosevelt.)
   What is the name of Jefferson's home?   **Monticello, in Virginia**
   What is the name of Washington's home?   **Mt. Vernon, in Virginia**
   Where can you find the Liberty Bell?   **Philadelphia, Pennsylvania**
   In what state are Yosemite and Sequoia National Parks?   **California**
   Where are the Ozark mountains?   **Missouri**
   What is Florida's famous swampland called?   **The Everglades**
   In what state are Bryce Canyon and Zion National Parks?   **Utah**
   Mt. St. Helen's volcano is in what state?   **Washington**
   In what national park is the famous geyser Old Faithful?   **Yellowstone**
   Where is Crater Lake?   **Oregon**
   The San Juan Capistrano Mission is in which state?   **California**
   What is the best known honeymoon spot in the country?   **Niagara Falls**
   The Mardi Gras takes place in what city?   **New Orleans**
   You will be given a flower necklace and a kiss when you arrive in what state?   **Hawaii**
   Pike's Peak is in what state?   **Colorado**

4. **World Vacation Spots.**

   What is the only human-built structure that can be seen from the moon?   **Great Wall of China**
   Where can you ride on a gondola on the canals?   **Venice, Italy**
   Where will you see kangaroos, wallabys, and koalas?   **Australia**
   Where are the pyramids?   **Egypt**

The Acropolis is high on a hill in which city? **Athens, Greece**

What is the land of windmills, tulips, and dikes? **Holland (The Netherlands)**

Pasta is a favorite food in which country? **Italy**

What city has a tall building that leans over? **Pisa, Italy—The Leaning Tower**

The Arc de Triomph is in which city? **Paris, France**

Mt. Fujiyama is in what country? **Japan**

The Rock of Gibraltar is a British possession but is next to which country? **Spain**

Mt. Vesuvius is in which city in Italy? **Naples**

The Taj Mahal is in what country? **India**

In what city is Buckingham Palace? **London, England**

Charles Boyer said "Let me take you to the Casbah"; where is it? **Algiers**

The Cape of Good Hope is at the bottom of which continent? **Africa**

The Sistine Chapel is in which city? **The Vatican, which is within Rome, Italy**

Monte Carlo is a resort in which small country? **Monaco**

What is the longest river in the world and where is it? **The Nile in Africa**

The Panama Canal is in which part of the Americas? **Central America**

5. **Swimsuits**. Discuss swimsuit styles during this century. Show pictures of swimsuits from different decades. (Check *Good Old Days* magazines, old and new Sears catalogs, library books about fashions or about the history of the Miss America pageant, old *Look* or *Life* magazines.) Ask the participants to describe the swimsuits that they wore as children, as young people, and as adults. Show pictures of current styles in swimsuits—check early summer issues of stylish women's magazines (such as *Comopolitan* or *McCall's*), swimsuit advertisements, or clothing catalogs. (*This Fabulous Century*, 1920-1930, has a photo of the swimsuit competition of an early Miss America pageant.)

6. **Trips**. Ask each person to tell about one of their memorable vacations or trips. You could ask them, in advance of the session, to bring any mementoes they might have about their trip or ask families for some information or mementoes of trips their family took together. You could find out from several participants, in advance, what place they would like to talk about and then try to find a picture to show the other participants at the session. Share something about one of your own trips or vacations.

7. **Accommodations**. A good place to stay can make or break a vacation. Encourage the participants, through discussion, to share their experiences about guest accommodations. Ask them if any remember the best hotel in which they ever slept, what the early motels were like, what it was like to stay in a guest house or tourist home, if any of them stayed in tents or trailers when they travelled, if they always stayed with relatives or friends. Ask them if they remember the cost of hotels in the 1920s or the 1930s. Give them a sample of hotel prices today. (Check AAA travel books.) (The Clark Gable/Claudette Colbert comedy movie "It Happened One Night" has a famous scene that takes place in a motel.)

8. **Travel Today**. Tell the participants about today's motor homes or recreation vehicles. You can get color brochures from local dealers to show.

9. **Vacation Spots Today**. Invite a travel agent to come and talk about the most popular vacation spots today, bringing as many visual aids as possible. You could ask the agent to concentrate on state or national places.

10. **Local Vacation Spots**. If you live near a particular vacation spot (beach, national park, monument, resort), ask a representative from there to come and talk to your group, bringing as many visual aids or objects to share as possible. Ask the participants to share their experiences of being there.

11. **Related Activity of particular male interest**. Invite an avid fisherman to come and talk about fishing, fishing equipment, and favorite fishing spots. Encourage the participants to share their fishing experiences.

12. **Related Activity**. If the participants are particularly interested in one country to visit, plan a "vacation of the mind." Announce that you will be "cruising" to a particular city or country. Give a bon voyage party (with champagne, cruise ship sound effects, ship decorations, travel songs) and "set sail," planning to "arrive" at your destination on a certain day, two to three days later. On your "arrival" day, plan several special events that will give the participants the flavor of the country, e.g., a slide show or movie about the country, someone knowledgeable to talk about the place, a meal of typical food from the country, or a group that will perform native dances or music or that will model native costumes. (Our nursing home has had successful "cruises" to a German Oktoberfest, a Hawaiian luau, and a Jamaican folk festival.)

DISCUSSION

1. Have any of you ever been given a trip as a gift? Where did you go?

2. Where did you go for honeymoons?

3. How often did people take vacations or go on trips when you were young?

4. How many of you prefer the beach to the mountains for a vacation? How many prefer the mountains? Why?

5. Have any of you had any unusual experiences with customs agents?

6. Have any of you ever been to any health spas like Roosevelt's Warm Springs, Georgia? Tell us about it.

7. Can any of you share with us the funniest memory you have of a vacation or trip?

VAUDEVILLE

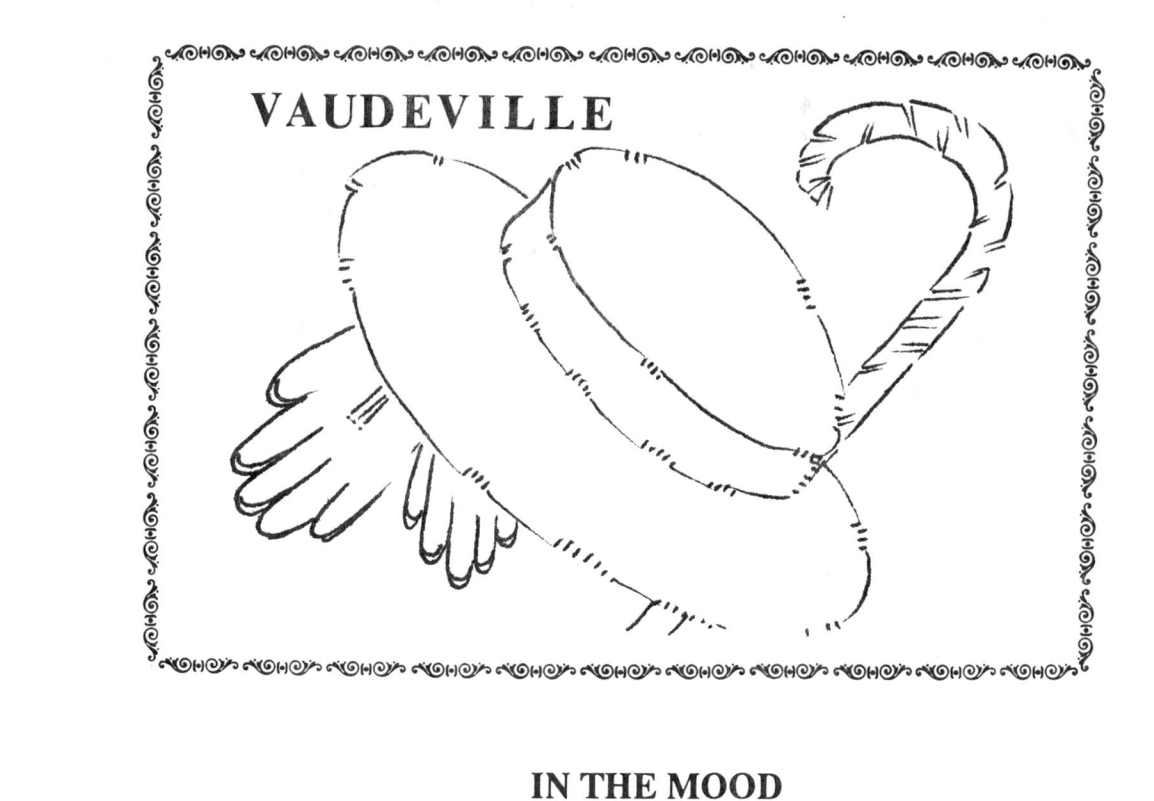

IN THE MOOD

Music Possibilities

1. Play or sing any of these songs that were first popularized on the vaudeville stage:

   "By the Light Of the Silv'ry Moon"   "School Days"
   "In the Shade Of the Old Apple Tree"   "After the Ball"
   "In My Merry Oldsmobile"   "Sweet Adeline"
   "Sidewalks Of New York"   "Sweet Rosie O'Grady"
   "Wait 'Til the Sun Shines, Nellie"   "Smiles"
   "Let the Rest Of the World Go By"   "The Band Played On"
   "Down By the Old Mill Stream"   "Shine On, Harvest Moon"
   "Let Me Call You Sweetheart"   "I Want a Girl"
   "When Irish Eyes Are Smiling"   "I Wonder Who's Kissing Her Now"

2. There are some good recordings of songs from vaudeville. Look for these:

   "Six Decades of American Popular Song," Smithsonian Institution (See Appendix A.)
   "Vaudeville Ladies" and "Ziegfeld Productions of 1919-1928," tapes from Presta Sounds
   "Vaudeville - Songs Of the Great Ladies Of the Musical Stage," Nonesuch Records

Visual Possibilities

1. Props from the vaudeville stage: skimmer (hat), cane, easel with the name of an "act" on it, a long crooked pole (used for pulling an act off the stage.)

2. Pictures of notable vaudeville stars or those stars who got their start in vaudeville. Examples:

Fred and Adele Astaire	Fanny Brice	Mae West
Nora Bayes	Lillian Russell	George M. Cohan
Weber & Fields	Harrigan & Hart	Eddie Foy
Burns & Allen	Eddie Cantor	George Jessel
Ray Bolger	Eleanor Powell	Marx Brothers
Bert Wheeler	Al Jolson	Harry Lauder
Florenz Ziegfeld	W.C. Fields	Ed Wynn
Will Rogers	Jack Benny	Marilyn Miller
Dolly Sisters	Milton Berle	Bill "Bojangles" Robinson
Pat Rooney	Bert Lahr	Ann Pennington

(Look for pictures in *This Fabulous Century*, as well as books about vaudeville, radio, and movies.)

ACTIVITIES

1. **Recordings**. If you have radio recordings of any of the stars mentioned in Visual Possibilities, play short excerpts and let the participants guess who the star is.

2. **Pictures**. Pass around any pictures you have and encourage everyone to reminisce about the people they see. Examples: Do any of you remember who this is? Did any of you ever see this person perform on the vaudeville circuit?

3. **Theaters**. If there are any old theaters still standing in your town, take pictures of them and share with the participants. Encourage them to share their memories of what they remember seeing there or in other towns. (Chicago had the Majestic Theater, San Francisco had the Orpheum, Boston had the Gaiety. There were also Vaudeville Circuits, in which a company in New York managed the theaters in small cities and booked the acts. Two major circuits at one time were the Proctor Circuit and the Radio-Keith-Orpheum Circuit.)

4. **Songs**. Sing together some of the songs listed in Music Possibilities. Ask the participants if any remember where they first heard it. If you have a good singer and accompanist, or recordings, you could play the verses of a song and let the participants guess what the chorus is, then all sing it together. Here are some good songs for that:

"Take Me Out To the Ballgame"	"After the Ball"
"Shine On, Harvest Moon"	"School Days"
"Meet Me In St. Louis"	"The Bowery"
"Wait 'Til the Sun Shines, Nellie"	"The Band Played On"

A good book for songs is Dover Publication's *Take Me Out to the Ball Game and other Favorite Song Hits 1906-1908*. This book has some good novelty vaudeville numbers that could be used for putting on a vaudeville show. (See Activity #7. Also, look in the library for song collections from the "Gay 90s" or the "Gaslight Era.")

5. **Speaker**. If you live in a city large enough to have had a vaudeville house, you might have someone living in your city, or even the nursing home, who was actively involved in the shows. Invite that person to come and share memories of it. (Check with your local musicians' union.)

6. **Related Activity**. Show some 1930s movies that were based on vaudeville acts, such as the Marx Brothers' "Animal Crackers" and "The Cocoanuts." Show "The Sunshine Boys," a movie about two old vaudeville stars.

7. **Related Activity**. Have your staff put on a vaudeville show. Some of the participants might be able to be a part of it, too. Here are some suggestions for putting on the show:

   A. It is important that your administrator support it. Staff will join in more readily if the administrative staff is enthusiastic and becomes a part of it.

   B. Some acts lend themselves to the use of a curtain for setting up. If you decide to have a curtain, enlist the help of the maintenance department to set it up. A simple one could be made with sheets, hung on a wire and strung across the room.

   C. It will be most successful if there are representatives from each department and shift. Maybe someone from each department could act as a talent scout for that department.

   D. For a large audience (30 or more), a microphone and amplifier of some kind is essential. If you can't afford to buy one, maybe you could borrow one from a staff or family member.

   E. Songs, pantomimes, simple skits, or dances work the best. Comic monologs are usually hard for the participants to hear and understand unless you have a very good microphone and a performer who speaks slowly and clearly.

   F. Put each act's name on a large poster on an easel to the side of the "stage" before each act performs.

   G. The acts can be quite varied. If a few of the acts have a staff member taking on the persona of a vaudeville star and performing a number that person made famous, it will be more meaningful and fun for the participants.

   Here are some ideas that have worked in shows of which I have been a part:

   Judy Garland: singing "Over the Rainbow," wearing hair in braids and holding a dog.

   Marlene Dietrich: singing "La Vie en Rose" or "Lilli Marlene"; a glamour woman in a blonde wig, with a cigarette in a holder, and singing in a low voice. She could be the MC for the show, introducing the acts.

   Nora Bayes: 1900s vaudeville star, in long, Victorian dress, pompadour hair style, and large hat; singing any of the songs listed earlier. (The verses that go with the songs add a lot to the performance.) Novelty numbers are the most fun, such as "The Bird on Nellie's Hat," "Poor John," "I Don't Care," or "Yip-I-Addy-I-Ay."

Billie Holiday: wearing a flower in her hair and simple evening dress and singing a blues song, like "Good Morning, Heartache" or "God Bless the Child."

Carmen Miranda: wearing a peasant blouse, flowery long skirt, long beads, and a hat with fruit on it; singing or dancing to a rhumba, cha-cha, or another Latin American rhythmic dance. If you can find a recording of Carmen Miranda, the song could be pantomimed.

The Charleston: two or more staff members dressed in flapper costumes and dancing the Charleston.

Shirley Temple: curly wig and little girl clothes, short socks, and Mary Jane shoes; singing "On the Good Ship Lollipop."

Mae West: wearing a tight evening dress, feather boa, long blonde wig, and big hat; telling suggestive stories and jokes, sitting on laps, singing a song such as "Frankie and Johnny." She could be the MC for the show, introducing the acts.

Louella Parsons: dressed in matronly clothes with a big hat; telling all the latest Hollywood (or facility) gossip.

DISCUSSION

1. Was there a vaudeville house in your town? Where was it? Who do you remember seeing there?

2. Did your family approve of vaudeville?

3. Did any of you go to vaudeville shows regularly? What was it like? Do any of you remember what it cost to see a show?

4. Have any of you ever appeared in an act or any kind of production? Tell us about it.

VOICES FROM THE PAST

IN THE MOOD

Music Possibilities - For this particular program, make a special effort to have original recordings if you can find them.

1. Collection of 1920s and 1930s songs, sung by the original artist.

2. An old radio show, particularly one with several performers, e.g., the Kate Smith, Eddie Cantor, or Bing Crosby shows.

3. A recording of a famous speech by someone such as Franklin Roosevelt, a collection of political speeches, or a famous comedian or humorist such as Will Rogers.

Visual Possibilities - Have as many pictures as you can find of famous personalities who were known for a particular quotation. (See list under Activity #4.) You can display pictures in the activity room or give a picture to each person who attends.

ACTIVITIES

1. **Voices**. If you have a recording with a collection of stars performing, or of speeches, play excerpts and see if the residents can recognize the personalities by their voices. Suggestions:

Katherine Hepburn	Kate Smith	Ingrid Bergman	Bob Hope
Humphrey Bogart	Jimmy Stewart	Cary Grant	Henry Fonda
Jack Benny	Jimmy Cagney	Burns and Allen	Bing Crosby
Louis Armstrong	Eleanor Roosevelt	Any of our presidents	

2. **Speeches.** If you have a record of famous speeches from 1920-1950, play excerpts and have the participants guess who is speaking.

3. **Pictures.** If you have pictures to pass around, ask the participants to guess who the personality is and a quote for which that person was noted, giving hints as needed.

4. **Quotations.** Give a quote and have the group, or individuals, guess who said it. After each answer is given, you could ask the participants if they remember when they first heard it, to whom it was being said, and the circumstances. Examples:

"Frankly, my dear, I don't give a damn."
   Rhett Butler to Scarlett O'Hara in "Gone With the Wind"
"Everybody wants to get into de act."
   Jimmy Durante
"I want to be alone."
   Greta Garbo
"Well, I'll be a dirty bird."
   George Gobel
"This is another fine mess you've gotten me into."
   Oliver Hardy to Stan Laurel
"You ain't heard nothing yet, folks."
   Al Jolson
"On, King! On, you huskies."
   Sergeant Preston
"What a revoltin' development this is."
   Chester Riley in "The Life of Riley"
"When the going gets tough, the tough get going."
   Knute Rockne
"I never met a man I didn't like."
   Will Rogers
"Come up and see me sometime."
   Mae West
"Heigh ho, everybody."
   Rudy Vallee
"So long until tomorrow."
   Lowell Thomas
"I got a million of 'em."
   Jimmy Durante
"Now cut that out."
   Jack Benny
"Here's looking at you, kid."
   Humphrey Bogart to Ingrid Bergman in "Casablanca"
"Gotta straighten out that closet one of these days."
   Fibber McGee
"Here he is, the one, the only—Groucho."
   George Fenneman, introducing Groucho on "You Bet Your Life"

"I don't mind where people make love, so long as they don't do it in the street and frighten the horses."
    Mrs. Patrick Campbell, British actress

"Genius is one percent inspiration and ninety-nine percent perspiration."
    Thomas Alva Edison (1932)

"Any customer can have a car painted any color he wants so long as it is black."
    Henry Ford (1909)

"What this country needs is a good 5-cent cigar."
    Vice President Thomas Marshall (1920)

"Check and double-check."
    "Amos 'n Andy" radio show

"Round and round she goes and where she stops, nobody knows."
    Major Bowes, "Original Amateur Hour" (radio)

"Ah yes, there's good news tonight."
    Gabriel Heatter, radio newscaster

"Tain't funny, McGee."
    Molly McGee, "Fibber McGee and Molly"

"He'd rather be right than president."
    Al Smith's presidential slogan

"I have nothing to offer but blood, toil, tears and sweat."
    Winston Churchill (1940)

"I do not choose to run for President in 1928."
    Calvin Coolidge (1927)

"I have found it impossible to carry the heavy burden of responsibility and to discharge my duties as King as I would wish to do without the help and support of the woman I love."
    King Edward VIII (1936, on abdicating the British throne)

"Let me assert my firm belief that the only thing we have to fear is fear itself."
    Franklin D. Roosevelt (1933 inaugural speech)

"The world must be made safe for democracy."
    Woodrow Wilson (1917)

5. **Tongue Twisters**. Ask the participants to try some tongue twisters together. Ask if they remember any others. Examples:

- "Rubber baby buggy bumpers."
- "She sells seashells by the seashore."
- "One slick snake slid down the slippery slue."
- "Peter Piper picked a peck of pickled peppers,
   A peck of pickled peppers Peter Piper picked."

6. **Memorizing**. Giving recitations or doing monologs was a popular way of entertainment on vaudeville and in the home in the days before radio. Ask the participants what they memorized when growing up. Some may remember lines of a poem or monolog they memorized when younger and would be willing to say them. You could read a famous poem like "Casey at the Bat" or the whole group could say something well-known together. Examples: Twenty-Third Psalm; Gettysburg Address; Lord's Prayer; Pledge of Allegiance; Preamble to the Constitution.

7. **Speaker.** Invite a local politican or a speechwriter to come to your facility to talk about the preparation that goes into writing and making speeches.

8. **Related Activity.** Show a movie having a political speech in it, such as "Mr. Smith Goes to Washington" or "State of the Union."

9. **Related Activity.** If you have a reading group, read some of Will Rogers' speeches or monologs. The humor is still funny today. (There are collections available in libraries or used bookstores.)

DISCUSSION

1. Have any of you ever given any speeches? Tell us about it. Did you like doing it?

2. Have any of you ever been a toastmaster or toastmistress and had to introduce a speaker? Do you remember the occasion? Did you ever tell a joke as part of your duties?

3. Were any of you afraid of speaking before groups? What did you do about it?

In this session, some of the discussion can come as a part of Activity #4, particularly those quotes that were in a newsworthy speech (the last five quotes.) You can ask the participants if they remember hearing the speech the first time it was made (or reading about it in the newspaper) and what impact it may have had on them at the time. The participants' political leanings may be reflected in the discussion.

You could end the session by reading a well-known poem or by telling a toastmaster's joke. (Look in the library for a book about toastmasters or a book of comic monologs.)

WEDDINGS

IN THE MOOD

Music Possibilities

1. Traditional wedding songs: "Oh, Promise Me," Bridal Chorus from "Lohengrin" ("Here Comes the Bride"), "O Perfect Love," "I Love You Truly," "Ich Liebe Dich" (Grieg), "Because," "Wedding March" (Mendelssohn).

2. Popular songs about weddings and marriage. Examples:

    "For Me and My Gal"
    "Yes Sir, That's My Baby"
    "Winter Wonderland"
    "The Girl That I Marry" (from "Annie Get Your Gun")
    "Sunrise, Sunset" (from "Fiddler On the Roof")
    "Come To Me, Bend To Me" (from "Brigadoon")
    "Put On Your Old Grey Bonnet"
    "Hawaiian Wedding Song"
    "Anniversary Song"
    "An Ordinary Couple" (from "The Sound of Music")
    "I Want a Girl"
    "My Cup Runneth Over" and "I Do, I Do" (from "I Do, I Do")
    "Get Me To the Church on Time" (from "My Fair Lady")
    "Wedding Bells Are Breaking Up That Old Gang of Mine"

2. Organ recital, such as would be typical before a wedding.

3. Presta Sounds tape, "Wedding Bells." (See Appendix A.)

Down Memory Lane 125

Visual Possibilities - *Modern Bride* magazines; pictures of brides from different eras; display of bridal dresses, veils, garters (staff members may be willing to bring in their wedding dresses to show); drawing of a multi-tiered wedding cake; figurines from the top of a cake.

ACTIVITIES

1. **Fashion Show**. Ask several staff members and/or family members to wear their wedding dresses to show the participants. You could have an M.C. describe each dress and/or you could ask each model to say a few words about her dress and her wedding.

2. **Photographs**. Ask the participants if they have a keepsake or picture from their wedding, honeymoon, or early marriage that they could bring to the group to share. Also, ask the participants to come with a story to share about their wedding or about the wedding of a close friend or relative. Some staff members also might be willing to bring a keepsake or picture to share that would, in turn, stimulate a participant to remember something.

3. **Customs**. Ask the participants to complete the following American wedding customs and ask if any of them followed that particular custom. Then ask them if they used or know of any others. Many ethnic groups have wedding customs that are unique to them.

>A bride's dress color should be. . .**white**.
>Brides are to wear. . .**something old, something new, something borrowed, something blue**.
>Catching the bride's bouquet means. . .**you will marry next**.
>Before the wedding, it's unlucky if the groom sees the bride wearing. . .**her wedding dress**.
>We throw rice on a newly married couple for. . .**fertility**.
>If a bride wears the wedding dress that her mother wore. . .**she will be lucky**.
>It is unlucky for a new bride to be carried across the. . .**threshold of her new home**.
>What should you tie to the back of a newlywed couple's car to ward off bad luck? **Tin cans**
>Who should cut and eat the first piece of wedding cake? **The bride and groom together**.
>It's bad luck to be a bridesmaid how many times? **Three**
>It's unlucky for a bride and groom to see each other. . .**on the wedding day before the ceremony**.
>If a bride sees herself fully dressed in a mirror before the wedding. . .**it's unlucky**.
>What are shotgun weddings? **A forced wedding, usually because the bride is pregnant**

4. **Just for Fun**. Here are some rather obscure wedding superstitions:

>A bride will be lucky if she gets married in old shoes.
>A bride will be unlucky if she gets married wearing green, unless she's Irish.
>It's lucky if a cat sneezes in the bride's home on the day before a wedding.
>If a stitch is added to the bridal dress right before the bride leaves for the church, it's good luck.
>It's lucky if a chicken is made to cackle in the home of newlyweds.
>If a married woman loses her wedding ring, she will lose her husband.
>It's unlucky if a pig crosses the path of a wedding party.

5. **Famous Couples in History.** Ask the participants to name famous couples in history. When they have remembered all they can, then use the couples on the following list which weren't named. Give the name of one member of the couple and let the participants guess the other member.

Antony - Cleopatra	Mary Pickford - Douglas Fairbanks, Buddy Rogers
Romeo - Juliet	Eddie Cantor - Ida
Fibber McGee - Molly	Jack Benny - Mary Livingstone
Clark Gable - Carole Lombard	Franklin Roosevelt - Eleanor Roosevelt
Scarlett O'Hara - Rhett Butler	Dagwood - Blondie
Humphrey Bogart - Lauren Bacall	George Burns - Gracie Allen
Nelson Eddy - Jeanette MacDonald	Spencer Tracy - Katherine Hepburn

6. **Wedding Songs.** Invite a singer to perform two or three traditional weddings songs and two or three contemporary wedding songs. Ask the participants to share their memories of the music they used in their weddings. Ask if anyone has any favorite love song. The soloist or your group could sing some of these songs; for example, "I Love You Truly" or "Let Me Call You Sweetheart."

7. **Wedding Etiquette.** Using *Miss Manners' Guide to Excruciatingly Correct Behavior* (available in libraries and bookstores), read letters to Miss Manners on wedding etiquette. Ask the participants how they would answer the questions and then read Miss Manners' answers. (Most of these deal with today's tricky etiquette problems in a way which is both correct and usually humorous.)

8. **Related Activity.** If you have several participants who are interested in drama, you could act out a mock wedding, using the traditional wedding service and ending with a simple reception. The more people who join in, the more fun it will be. Don't forget these parts: preacher, bride, groom, ring bearer, flower girl, soloist, organist, mother and father of the bride and of the groom, attendants, wedding guests, photographer. Some of the participants might have some ideas for making it humorous or they might want to do it "straight."

DISCUSSION

1. Can some of you share when your anniversary is? Do you remember what year you were married?

2. Did any of you elope? How did you go about it?

3. Can any of you remember what your wedding dress looked like? Describe it for us.

4. Did anyone have a wedding that was untraditional for that time? How was it different?

5. Can some of you share what kind of reception you had after your wedding?

6. Did anyone go to Niagara Falls for your honeymoon? What were some other good honeymoon spots?

7. Did anything funny happen at your wedding or reception or on your honeymoon? (Ask this question early in the session so participants can think about it before answering.)

End the session by singing "I Love You Truly" and serving punch and a white sheet cake.

IN THE MOOD

Music Possibilities - Popular songs about working. Examples:

"Whistle While You Work"	"Workin' On the Railroad"
"Heigh-ho, Heigh-ho"	"Ten Cents a Dance"
"Ballad Of John Henry"	"Union Maid"
"Talkin' Union Blues"	"Joe Hill"
"Ol' Man River"	"Bread and Roses"
"Nice Work If You Can Get It"	"Drill, Ye Tarriers, Drill"
"Fifteen Years On the Erie Canal"	"The Anvil Chorus," from the opera "Il Trovatore"

Visual Possibilities

1. Work hats - train conductor's cap, cowboy hat, hard hat, nurse's cap, baseball cap, pilot's hat, football helmet, police officer's hat, armed forces hats, fire fighter's hat, etc. (To find these, check thrift shops or ask at local nursery schools, which usually keep a supply of hats.)

2. Pictures of people working at different jobs. Norman Rockwell painted many of these and collections of his drawings would be in the library. Also, see Dover Publications' *Men at Work* and *Women at Work*.

3. Tools associated with specific jobs. See Activity #2 below.

4. Post on the wall the following proverbs about work:

"A man works from sun to sun but a woman's work is never done."
"Anything worth doing is worth doing well."
"Behind every successful man is a woman."

"Jack of all trades and master of none."
"Another day, another dollar."
"All work and no play makes Jack a dull boy."

ACTIVITIES

1. **Hats**. Pass around the hats and ask the participants to identify what profession or group would wear which hat. Ask them if they or their spouses ever wore any of these hats or any other distinctive ones.

2. **Tools**. Collect tools associated with specific professions and ask the participants to name the job. Or more simply, you could just name a tool and ask with which job it is associated. (Showing the tools is usually more effective but takes more preparation.) Examples:

　　stethoscope - doctor, nurse
　　grass clippers - gardener
　　hammer and nails - carpenter
　　hoe - farmer
　　metronome - musician
　　beaker - chemist
　　whistle - police officer, lifeguard
　　plunger, pipes - plumber
　　blueprints - draftsman, architect
　　pills - pharmacist
　　legal pad - lawyer
　　paintbrush - artist, painter
　　Bible - minister, rabbi
　　scissors and comb - barber
　　fish net - fisherman
　　road map - taxi driver, geographer
　　deck of cards - gambler
　　watch or necklace - jeweler

　　ledger paper - bookkeeper, accountant
　　wooden spoon - cook, chef
　　wrench - auto mechanic, plumber
　　steno book - stenographer, secretary
　　needle and thread - seamstress, tailor
　　chalk and eraser - teacher, professor
　　baby bottle, diaper - parent
　　wire, electrical parts - electrician
　　book - librarian, printer, bookseller
　　shovel - road worker, forester, gardener
　　typewriter - writer, secretary
　　apron - homemaker, cook, soda jerk, waitress
　　telephone - operator, telephone installer
　　newspaper - reporter, editor, paper deliverer
　　money - banker, bookkeeper, cashier
　　microphone - announcer, speaker, singer
　　shoe - shoemaker, shoe repair person, dancer

3. **"What Was My Line?"** Recreate the popular old game show "What's My Line?" Ask several participants to be contestants and let the others guess what each contestant's former occupation was. (It could be any job held by that person during his/her life.) If you have three to four participants who would be able to ask astute questions and remember all the clues, you could have a panel to do the guessing, opening it up to the audience if they were stumped. Suggest to the guessers that they start with questions that are broad and that get more specific as more information is known. Suggested rules:

　　A. Before starting, tell the guessers if the occupation was a service or if it dealt in a product.
　　B. All questions asked of each contestant must be able to be answered by "yes" or "no."
　　C. If a panel is asking the questions, each panelist can continue to ask questions as long as the answer is "yes." As soon as the contestant gives a "no" answer, go on to the next panelist.
　　D. After 10 "no" answers, the contestant has won. You could give each contestant a dime for each "no" answer.

4. **Working**. Studs Terkel has written a fascinating book called *Working* in which he interviewed workers from all walks of life. You, or participants, could read excerpts from the book, particularly the sections about workers who had the same occupations as some of the participants. You could ask those participants if they felt the same about their jobs.

5. **Occupations**. Ask each participant to say a few words about his or her main occupation in life, place of work, and daily routine.

6. **Jobs Today**. Share with the participants what jobs are in demand today and will be for the next few years: health care workers, computer specialists, engineers, office workers. Computers are the wave of the future in almost every profession. If you have access to a computer, give a brief demonstration of some of its capabilities (word processor, games, spreadsheets, graphics, etc.). Many children's "toys" today are electronic marvels, with computer chips, too. One of those toys, like "Speak and Spell," could be shown. You could also show a computer floppy disk that is bad and can be taken apart.

7. **Nursing Home Jobs**. Ask someone from each department in the nursing home to say a few words about his or her job duties.

8. **Related Activity**. Show the movie "Desk Set," a humorous 1950s film about an office's first experience with a computer. It stars Katherine Hepburn and Spencer Tracy.

DISCUSSION

Ask the participants to share their memories about the following aspects of working:

1. First paid job - what, where, what age, pay, first boss

2. Working hours - how many hours in a typical day or week, weekend work

3. Payday - how paid and when, wages, raises, any benefits

4. Work whistles - when whistles were blown

5. Being self-employed - what business, where

6. Working women - what jobs were open to women, any unusual or pioneering jobs held by a female resident, career or temporary, working during the world wars

7. Jobs held by father and mother - visiting a parent's work place; helping with a family business

8. Unions - involvement, strikes, and other protests. (This could be a very sensitive subject because there were some bitter union struggles, especially during the 1930s.)

9. Retirement - when, after how many years, celebrations

10. After retirement - how time was spent (travel, hobbies, etc.)

APPENDIX A - ANNOTATED RESOURCE LIST

General

1. Libraries - Books, records, films, old Sears or Wards catalogs. Check the juvenile books, as well as adult. Some libraries hold periodic sales of old books, too.

2. Used book or record stores - Look for Americana or nostalgia books, old *Look* or *Life* magazines, posters, comic books, records, sheet music, old Sears or Wards catalogs.

3. Antique shops - You might be able to rent or borrow some appropriate objects for a session.

4. Estate or yard sales - Especially good for nostalgic objects if the sale is from the home of a retired person.

Specific

Companies

1. **Dover Publications, Inc.**, 31 East 2nd St., Mineola, NY 11501. This company carries low-priced books on many subjects. The most useful for reminiscence groups are those with historic photographs of famous people and events. They also have an old Montgomery Ward catalog. Specific book suggestions are listed with the appropriate chapter in this book.

2. **Giant Photo, Inc.**, Box 406, Rockford, IL 61105. This company, aiming at the education market, sells inexpensive posters and pictures on many subjects.

3. **Le Ann Publishing Company**, 4550 Quebec Avenue North, Minneapolis, MN 55428. Their specialty is large-print songbooks and hymnbooks for use with seniors, *Sing Along Song Books*.

4. **Medical and Activities Sales Company**, P.O. Box 4068, Omaha, NE 68104. This company carries a variety of activity books and equipment, including photocopies of some good books that are out of print, such as *Discussion Topics for Oldsters*.

5. **M & N International**, 4170 Grove Ave., Gurnee, IL 60031. Party goods and decorations, travel posters.

6. **Paradise Products**, P.O. Box 568, El Cerrito, CA 94530. Party goods and decorations, travel posters - half price to institutions.

7. **Popplers Music Store**, 123 Demers Avenue, P.O. Box 398, Grand Forks, ND 58206. They sell a variety of different songbooks of popular songs.

8. **Potentials Development**, 775 Main Street, Buffalo, NY 14203. This company specializes in inexpensive books for activities directors in nursing homes. The "Quizz Whizz" packets are good.

9. **Presta Sounds**, P.O. Box 4351, Macon, GA 31208. This company specializes in selling cassettes of old radio shows plus making cassettes of music programs on a variety of subjects that appeal to seniors, such as "Exercise with Fred Astaire," "Vaudeville Ladies," "Dance Party a la 20s," etc. The company will also make up special tapes on request.

10. **Publishers Central Bureau**, One Champion Avenue, Avenel, NJ 07001. This is a company that deals mainly in "remainders," books that publishers have stopped selling. They have nostalgia books and recordings, plus books on every other topic imaginable. You have to read through their catalog carefully, but there are some good resources here.

11. **Rhythm Band**, P.O. Box 126, Fort Worth, TX 76101. This company has large-print songbooks for seniors, entitled *Silver Tones Among the Gold*, as well as rhythm instruments.

12. **Vestal Press**, 320 N. Jensen Road, P.O. Box 97, Vestal, NY 13851. This is a book publisher and distributer of nostalgia items, particularly those related to entertainment. The catalog also carries a large selection of cassette recordings of player piano rolls, music boxes, and carousels.

Books, Records, Magazines

1. "**American Popular Song**," Smithsonian Recordings, P.O. Box 10230, Des Moines, IA 50336. This is a seven-record or four-cassette set of original recordings from 1910 to 1954. The Smithsonian has a variety of other special record collections, too.

2. *Chase's Calendar of Events*. This book lists events to celebrate for every day of the year, plus places to write for more information. There are several companies that carry it and libraries usually have copies of it in their Reference section. To order it directly from the publisher, write to Best Publications, Dept. C, 180 N. Michigan, Chicago, IL 60601.

3. *The Complete Unabridged Super Trivia Encyclopedia*, by Fred L. Worth, Brooke House Publishing, 1977. Almost any American trivia book could be helpful. In these books you can find lists of all sorts of interesting things.

4. *The Encyclopedia of Collectibles*, Time-Life Books, 1979. Available in libraries and used bookstores. These books have good color pictures of vintage objects.

5. *The Fun Encyclopedia*, by E.O. Harbin. Available from World Wide Games, Colchester, CT 06415. This is a good all-purpose book for recreation directors anywhere. It was out of print but has been recently updated and reissued. The original edition can still be found in libraries and used bookstores. The chapter on "Fun with Mental Games" is the most valuable for use with the programs in this book.

6. *Good Old Days* **magazine**, P.O. Box 11302, Des Moines, IA 50340. This is a good resource for pictures and old ads. It also has short, memory-sharing articles that are good for reading groups.

7. *The Great Song Thesaurus* by Roger Lax and Frederick Smith, Oxford University Press. This is a premier reference guide to American popular songs, with over 10,000 song titles indexed by year, composer, and subject.

8. *Ideals* **magazines**, Ideals Publishing Corporation, P.O. Box 148000, Nashville, TN 37214. These magazines are full of beautiful pictures and poetry; very useful in getting a discussion started.

9. *Keep Minds Alert*. This book is full of lists of things on many subjects and is written for use in nursing homes. It is available from Medical and Activities Sales Company (see address page 131) and from KMA Games Corporation, Box 443, Sac City, IA 50583.

10. *Let's Talk* by Elenore E. Ashworth, L'Anciana Press, 1065 Park Hills Rd., Berkeley, CA 94708. This is a book of remotivation programs for use in nursing homes. It's very easy to use and the programs are well planned.

11. *Memories, Dreams and Thoughts, A Guide to Mental Stimulation* by Jim Brennan, available from Publicare Press, P.O. Box 5758, Bossier City, LA 71171. It is full of mental stimulation games and questions for discussions; an excellent resource.

12. **Norman Rockwell books**. Norman Rockwell painted hundreds of pictures that captured the spirit and culture of America. There are many collections of his paintings available and if you can find one, it would be a valuable addition to your library. Publisher's Central Bureau has carried them; try used bookstores, too.

13. **Reader's Digest songbooks**, The Reader's Digest Association, Inc., Pleasantville, New York 10570. These ten books are a great source of sheet music for American popular songs. You can order the books directly from the company or sometimes find them in bookstores. (Reader's Digest has several record collections of popular songs, too.) Here are the names of the books:

> *Popular Songs That Will Live Forever*
> *Merry Christmas Songbook*
> *Country and Western Songbook*
> *Remembering Yesterday's Hits*
> *Children's Songbook*
> *Family Songbook of Faith and Joy*
> *Unforgettable Musical Memories*
> *Festival of Popular Songs*
> *Family Songbook*
> *Treasury of Best Loved Songs*

14. *This Fabulous Century*, Time-Life Books, 1969. This is a series of books on each one of the first six decades of the 20th century, plus one on the years 1870-1900. These books are out-of-print. However, most libraries have one or more copies and some used bookstores carry them. If you can get these books, they are a real treasure.

APPENDIX B - INDEX TO POPULAR SONGS

1892
After the Ball
Bicycle Built For Two
The Bowery

1894
The Sidewalks of New York

1895
America, the Beautiful
The Band Played On

1896
A Hot Time In the Old Town
Sweet Rosie O'Grady

1898
Because
Gypsy Love Song

1899
Hello! Ma Baby
Maple Leaf Rag
My Wild Irish Rose

1900
A Bird In a Gilded Cage

1901
Mighty Lak' a Rose

1902
Bill Bailey
In the Good Old Summertime
In the Sweet Bye and Bye

1903
Ida! Sweet As Apple Cider!
Sweet Adeline

1904
Give My Regards To Broadway
Meet Me In St. Louis
The Yankee Doodle Boy

1905
In My Merry Oldsmobile
Mary's a Grand Old Name
Wait 'Til the Sun Shines, Nellie

1906
Anchors Aweigh
I Love You, Truly
You're a Grand Old Flag

1907
The Glow-Worm
Harrigan
School Days

1908
Cuddle Up a Little Closer
Shine On, Harvest Moon

1909
By the Light of the Silv'ry Moon
I Wonder Who's Kissing Her Now?
Put on Your Old Grey Bonnet

1910
Ah! Sweet Mystery of Life
Come, Josephine, in My Flying Machine
Down by the Old Mill Stream
Let Me Call You Sweetheart

1911
Alexander's Ragtime Band
Good-night, Ladies
Oh, You Beautiful Doll

1912
It's a Long Way to Tipperary
Moonlight Bay
The Sweetheart of Sigma Chi
When Irish Eyes Are Smiling

1913
Ballin' the Jack
Danny Boy

The Old Rugged Cross
Peg O' My Heart
There's a Long, Long Trail
You Made Me Love You

1914
By the Beautiful Sea
St. Louis Blues
When You Wore a Tulip

1915
Keep the Home Fires Burning
Memories
The Old Gray Mare
Pack Up Your Troubles In Your Old Kit Bag
  and Smile, Smile, Smile

1916
I Ain't Got Nobody
Poor Butterfly
Pretty Baby

1917
For Me and My Gal
Hail, Hail the Gang's All Here
Oh Johnny, Oh Johnny, Oh!
Over There
Smiles
Will You Remember (Sweetheart)

1918
Beautiful Ohio
K-K-K-Katy
Till We Meet Again

1919
Alice Blue Gown
How Ya Gonna Keep 'Em Down on the Farm?
I'm Forever Blowing Bubbles
Swanee

1920
I'll Be With You In Apple Blossom Time
Look For the Silver Lining

1921
Ain't We Got Fun?
April Showers
I'm Just Wild About Harry
Ma, He's Making Eyes At Me
Second Hand Rose

1922
Carolina in the Morning
My Buddy
Toot, Toot, Tootsie

1923
Charleston
Yes! We Have No Bananas

1924
California, Here I Come!
The Man I Love
Rose-Marie
Tea For Two

1925
Alabamy Bound
Always
Five Foot Two, Eyes of Blue
I'm Sitting on Top of the World
If You Knew Susie
Show Me the Way to go Home
Sweet Georgia Brown
Yes Sir, That's My Baby

1926
Baby Face
The Birth of the Blues
Bye Bye Blackbird
The Desert Song
Gimme a Little Kiss
Someone to Watch Over Me
When the Red, Red, Robin

1927
The Best Things in Life are Free
Blue Skies
Can't Help Lovin' That Man
Funny Face
I'm Looking Over a Four-leaf Clover
Let a Smile Be Your Umbrella
Make Believe
Me and My Shadow
My Blue Heaven
Ol' Man River
Side By Side
Sometimes I'm Happy
Strike Up the Band
'Swonderful
The Varsity Drag

1928
Button Up Your Overcoat
Carolina Moon
Honey
I Can't Give You Anything But Love
I'll Get By
Lover, Come Back To Me
Makin' Whoopee!
Softly, As In a Morning Sunrise
When You're Smiling

1929
Ain't Misbehavin'
Am I Blue?
Happy Days Are Here Again
More Than You Know
Puttin' On the Ritz
Star Dust
Tiptoe Through the Tulips
Sunny Side Up

1930
Bidin' My Time
Body and Soul
On the Sunny Side Of the Street
Ten Cents a Dance
Walkin' My Baby Back Home
Would You Like To Take a Walk

1931
Goodnight, Sweetheart
I Found a Million Dollar Baby
I Love a Parade
Life Is Just a Bowl Of Cherries
Minnie the Moocher
Mood Indigo
When the Moon Comes Over the Mountain
Where the Blue Of the Night

1932
Brother, Can You Spare a Dime?
42nd Street
How Deep Is the Ocean?
Night and Day

1933
Did You Ever See a Dream Walking?
Easter Parade
Heat Wave
Inka Dinka Doo
Smoke Gets In Your Eyes
Sophisticated Lady
Stormy Weather
Who's Afraid Of the Big, Bad Wolf?
We're In the Money

1934
Blue Moon
The Continental
I Only Have Eyes for You
No! No! A Thousand Times No!
On the Good Ship Lollipop
Tumbling Tumbleweeds
Wagon Wheels
Winter Wonderland
You Oughta Be in Pictures
You're the Top

1935
Begin the Beguine
Cheek to Cheek
I'm Gonna Sit Right Down and Write Myself a Letter
I'm in the Mood for Love
The Lord's Prayer
Lullaby of Broadway
Red Sails in the Sunset
Summertime
Top Hat, White Tie, and Tails
When I Grow Too Old to Dream
You Are My Lucky Star

1936
It's De-Lovely
I've Got You Under My Skin
Pennies from Heaven
Stompin' at the Savoy

1937
Bei Mir Bist Du Schon
Blue Hawaii
The Donkey Serenade
A Foggy Day
In the Still of the Night
The Lady is a Tramp
Let's Call the Whole Thing Off
My Funny Valentine

1938
A-Tisket, A-Tasket
Falling in Love with Love
Flat Foot Floogie

I'll Be Seeing You
Jeepers Creepers
My Heart Belongs to Daddy
September Song
Two Sleepy People
You Must Have Been a Beautiful Baby

1939
All the Things You Are
Beer Barrel Polka
God Bless America
I'll Never Smile Again
Over the Rainbow
Three Little Fishies

1940
The Nearness of You
Taking a Chance On Love
When You Wish Upon a Star
You Are My Sunshine

1941
Blues In the Night
Chattanooga Choo Choo
Deep In the Heart Of Texas
I Don't Want To Walk Without You
White Cliffs Of Dover

1942
I'm Old-Fashioned
Jingle, Jangle, Jingle
Paper Doll
That Old Black Magic
This Is the Army
White Christmas

1943
Comin' In on a Wing and a Prayer
Mairsy Doats
Oh, What a Beautiful Mornin'
People Will Say We're In Love

1944
Ac-cent-tchuate the Positive
Don't Fence Me In
Rum and Coca-Cola
Sentimental Journey
Swinging on a Star

1945
If I Love You
It Might as Well be Spring
It's Been a Long, Long Time
Let It Snow
On the Atchison, Topeka, and the Santa Fe

1946
Anniversary Song
Come Rain or Come Shine
Doin' What Comes Naturally
The Girl That I Marry
How Are Things in Glocca Morra?
Now Is the Hour
Old Devil Moon
Tenderly
There's No Business Like Show Business
Zip-a-dee-doo-dah

1947
Heather on the Hill
There! I've Said It Again

1948
'A'—You're Adorable
Baby, It's Cold Outside
Buttons and Bows
Once in Love With Amy

1949
Bali Ha'i
Dear Hearts and Gentle People
Rudolph, the Red-nosed Reindeer
Some Enchanted Evening

Sources:

Popular Music: An Annotated Index of American Popular Songs, edited by Nat Shapiro, Adrian Press, Publisher

Variety Music Cavalcade, by Julius Mattfeld, Prentice-Hall, Publisher

APPENDIX C - QUIZ AND GAME INDEX

Advertisements
Slogans, 5
Sponsors, 5
Trademarks, 6

Advice
Common Sayings, 8
Intellectual Sayings, 8

American Popular Song
Addendum, 14
Lyrics Quiz, 13
Name That Tune, 11
Signature Songs, 11
Songs Associated with
 Historical Events, 12

Big Bands
Big Band Songs, 16
Big Band Trivia, 18
Instruments, 17
Slang, 19
Theme Songs, 18

Broadway Musicals
Association, 21
Broadway Songs, 21
Plots, 22

Childhood
Games, 25
Nursery Rhymes, 26
Stories, 26

Comedians
Comedy Partners, 30
Comedians' Trivia, 30
Quotations, 30

Dancing
Dance Trivia, 33

Fashions
"What Is It?", 37

The Funnies
Funnies Trivia, 41

Golden Age of Television
Television Trivia, 44

Home Sweet Home
Household Items, 48

Ice Cream Parlor
Ice Cream Treats, 52
The Soda Jerk, 52

Movies
Movie Trivia, 57

My Home Town
Song Title Quiz, 64

Needlework
Notions, 67

The News
Personalities, 71

Old-time Radio
Characters, 75
Introductions, 74
Theme Songs, 74

Opera
Opera Plots, 79
Opera Props, 79
Opera Stars, 78

Operetta
Operetta Trivia, 82

Pets
Animal Babies, 85
Animal Groups, 85
Notable Pets, 86

Roaring Twenties
People, 91
Slang, 90

Roosevelt
New Deal Programs, 95
People, 94
Popular Culture, 96

School Days
Arithmetic, 99
Foreign Languages, 101
History, 100
Spelling, 99

Shopping
Catalog Items, 104
Products, 104

Sports
Heroes, 107
Home Teams, 108
Sports, 108

Superstitions
Common Superstitions, 111

Vacations
American Vacation Spots, 114
World Vacation Spots, 114

Voices From the Past
Quotations, 122

Weddings
Customs, 126
Famous Couples, 127

Working
Tools, 129
"What Was My Line?", 129

138   *Down Memory Lane*